Designing and moderating workshops

Develop successful strategies and solutions in 5 steps

By Manuel Hausharter

Contents

Introduction: Difference Moderation and Presentation

Moderation & Presentation

A workshop is characterized by the fact that a group meets outside of the daily professional routine for an extended period of time to work together on solving a given task that can be implemented in the future in the daily work routine. Elsewhere, the pleasant atmosphere of a workshop invites participants to develop creative ideas, explore new avenues and develop a sense of belonging. Such a productive meeting is led by a facilitator. His or her task is to support the participants during the process and to visualize and document all steps on the way to the goal. A professional moderator thus motivates the participants to act together, but always remains in the background as an observer in terms of content. In addition, it is the moderator's responsibility to ensure that the communication he or she stimulates remains within the given framework, both thematically and in terms of time. A moderator can call himself successful if the solutions and measures developed are jointly supported and adopted. In addition, these results must be sustainable, i.e., they must have an effect beyond the workshop. If necessary, the support of a specialist can also be a sensible option. In contrast to moderation, a presentation does not require the active participation of the participants. Rather, the presenter is in the foreground. As a "sole entertainer", he or she primarily imparts knowledge, while the participants take on the passive role of observers. The presenter is aware from the outset that his central role means that he is constantly exposed to criticism from his audience. He or she must therefore succeed from the very beginning in picking up his or her audience and at the same time arousing so much interest that they follow him or her attentively to the end of his or her presentation. This is a very difficult and challenging task that requires a lot of personality and professionalism from the presenter. In contrast to a presentation, a workshop requires the active participation of the participants. Here, there is no primary transfer of knowledge. Rather, the focus is on working out joint strategies, solving problems, or imparting knowledge to each other. Precisely because there is no prepared transfer of knowledge, there is an opportunity for interaction between the participants, which in learning together should lead to new insights - the goal of every successful workshop.

Chapter 1: What makes a good facilitator? Our role as moderator

Workshop Definition & General

During a workshop, a group works intensively on a given topic with limited time. An important characteristic is the cooperative and at the same time moderated collaboration, which should lead to a jointly developed goal. Today, moderation is no longer understood as merely leading the discussion; rather, it is consciously used as an effective method to control communication within the working groups. The moderator no longer wants to be a pure discussion leader who controls and influences the course of the discussion. Rather, all participants should be encouraged by his participation to actively contribute to the development and design of a solution. Ideally, the creative cooperation between the group and the moderator will lead to a jointly developed result that can be understood by all participants, jointly supported and sustainably implemented. In reality, however, the practical implementation can often deviate from such an ideal case. For example, unsystematic discussion management, interpersonal conflicts and discussions that get out of hand can lead to completely opposite results. Valuable working time will then not be able to be used efficiently, urgently needed results will not be produced, and in the worst case, there is a threat of termination. It is hard to imagine the emotional state in which the participants of such an unproductive workshop leave. On the other hand, a scenario of this kind also makes it clear what a great responsibility the moderator has within a workshop on the way to working out common goals. A workshop will always be successful if the tasks are clearly distributed by the moderator and the responsibilities are regulated. The participants are responsible for the content of their contributions, while the moderator assumes responsibility for the process. At all times, the moderator keeps an eye on the timeline and structure of the process and is responsible for documenting the results. He or she accompanies the process professionally with the help of targeted questions and theses, which on the one hand maintain an active exchange of opinions, but on the other hand provide the participants with a fixed structure, i.e. a common thread. Whoever is entrusted with the responsible task of leading a workshop will certainly do everything in his power to avoid boredom and unproductive work. The basic prerequisite for this is a well-prepared and well thought-out moderation that is able to offer the participants structure, security and orientation. At the same time, structured moderation also requires sufficient leeway to be able to flexibly adapt to the different characters and individual circumstances at any time. It requires a great deal of empathy on the part of the moderator to involve each individual participant within a climate - free of any hierarchy - and to encourage them to participate actively. Ideally, however, the end result is a common pool of knowledge, competence and creativity that can be implemented effectively and sustainably through the acceptance of all participants.

KO criteria for the success of a workshop

To guarantee the success of a workshop, certain criteria must be met. For example, creative ideas can only lead to sustainable solutions if the problem to be worked on is relevant to all participants and actually leads to difficulties in real working life. In other words, all participants should be affected by the problem in some way and have an interest in finding a corresponding solution. Why else would participants be motivated to work on finding a solution? In this context, it is also important that the problem to be solved does not exceed a certain magnitude so that it can be mastered within the time-limited framework of a workshop. To solve the problem, you receive a clear assignment from the client. He determines the modalities, defines the purpose and specific objectives of the workshop and provides the necessary funds. Without him, there will be no workshop and he expects you to ensure that the working time of his employees and his money are well invested. In order to give the participants sufficient opportunity to prepare in advance, care should be taken to invite them in good time. At the latest when selecting the participants, the question arises as to whether they are authorized to make decisions at all on the basis of their position. And should decisions be made, is there then corresponding money available for the implementation of the goals and measures developed in the workshop? You as the moderator also make a significant contribution to the success of your workshop as an essential "criterion". You set the rules and make sure that they are adhered to. You always stay in the background, do not comment on the content in any way at any time, and instead skilfully steer the workshop by asking specific questions. In summary, it can be said at this point that without a clear mandate, without sufficient time, without appropriate participant selection, without motivation of the participants and without your self-understanding of the role of a moderator, a workshop will not succeed.

So what makes a professional facilitator?

But what are the qualities that make a facilitator a professional facilitator? A professional moderator is able to turn a motley group of people, who may not even know each other, into a team that develops the desire to work together to solve a problem - and to do so within a very limited period of time. A professional facilitator is so well prepared that the participants have the impression that nothing has been prepared and that the workshop actually runs all by itself. A professional facilitator sees himself as a kind of catalyst who has mastered the fine art of letting the group work undisturbed on a problem while placing himself in the background. As long as the group - in the opinion of the moderator - is on the right track, nothing will change in this position. Thus, the success of a facilitator can be defined quite clearly: If his preparation fulfills the objective of the workshop and the participants have the feeling that the solution has been found all by itself, then a moderator may call himself professional and chalk up this success accordingly.

What are the tasks of a professional moderator?

The moderator plans the workshop, is responsible for the organizational preparation and is primarily responsible for the overall process. During the planning phase, the clear definition of the workshop objective is one of his or her most important tasks. At the beginning of the workshop, it is the facilitator's task to introduce the participants to the topic. The rules that apply to the workshop must also be defined and accepted by the participants. In the further course, compliance with the rules and the "discreet" handling of rule violations will be his responsibility. The moderator is responsible for shaping the course of the conversation and ensuring a pleasant atmosphere for the discussion. It is his responsibility to steer the talks and discussions. At the same time, the moderator may not manipulate the discussions at any time, and comments on content are absolutely taboo. A moderator does not take sides, nor does he or she evaluate contributions to the discussion in any way. As a moderator, do you have the feeling that the discussion is going in a completely wrong direction or is not progressing at all? Then you must deliberately take a back seat. Instead of taking a position on the content, you can skillfully steer the conversation in the direction you want by formulating appropriate questions without the participants consciously noticing this. "Have you perhaps already thought about...?" After all, the fine art of moderation lies in guiding conversations in such a way that participants do not feel disturbed by your moderation. If you are the calming influence in the course of the workshop and never lose sight of the goal, trust can awake and the good feeling can arise that with you as moderator every job will be done - no matter what happens. One of your most difficult tasks as a facilitator will certainly be to motivate the participants. How committed will they be to the tasks you set them? The answer to this question depends largely on you, because fun in learning is a human trait that is basically in every one of your participants. Consequently, it is your task to bring out this desire to learn, to use existing potentials and to create a pleasant working atmosphere in which the participants can concentrate on the tasks set. A good moderator is also expected to have a great deal of sensitivity, because on the way to the goal there is only a fine line between being overchallenging on the one hand and underchallenging on the other, and the motivation of your participants stands and falls with both. One of the many responsible tasks of a moderator is the visualization and documentation of the results. This must be done clearly, comprehensibly and in understandable terms. In case of ambiguities, the moderator is available as a contact person at any time. Praise is also a factor that should not be underestimated. Provide constant immediate feedback throughout, not just one big final praise during the evaluation at the end of the workshop. In fact, you can plan your workshop to be exactly "praise-oriented" by preparing small tasks that allow for immediate and positive feedback on your part.

Conclusion: without a clear mission, sufficient time and motivated participants, a workshop will not be able to succeed. Your very personal attitude also contributes significantly to the success of the workshop. What basic competencies do you need as a moderator to be able to fulfill the tasks set for you calmly and professionally? Are you an organizational talent? Can you listen well, are you polite and have oodles of patience? Do you manage to remain neutral at all times, to keep a low profile, and yet exude an aura of authority that gets you heard? Do you have enough sensitivity to understand the different character traits of your participants and also to be able to interpret signals of non-verbal communication? Can you answer all these questions with a resounding "yes"?

Congratulations! Then nothing stands in your way of becoming a professional moderator.

Chapter 2: Preparing your moderation

The right preparation

Well thought-out preparation is the be-all and end-all of any successful workshop. In order to achieve the desired success, the concept and problem should already be clearly defined during planning. In addition, there is the organizational preparation, because a workshop requires sufficient time, adequate premises and a suitable selection of materials to provide visual support. In addition, a sound knowledge of moderation techniques, discussion rules or how to deal with heterogeneous group constellations will ensure that you lead your workshop confidently and successfully. Decisions and measures must be documented by you and subsequently sent to the participants in written form. This eliminates possible misunderstandings, removes ambiguities and also enables people who were not part of the workshop to be informed about all relevant processes and measures. Implementation can now begin before a results check can be carried out at a later date - the basis for this: The results you set down in writing. Preparation and moderation therefore do not just work "by the way", rather they are essential prerequisites for the successful implementation of your assignment. Well prepared, you can welcome the participants of your workshop in a relaxed manner, guide the working groups confidently and document constructive results professionally. Your personal red thread through workshop preparation
Clearly defined objectives

Before you start planning and implementing your workshop, the objectives and desired results must first be clearly defined. Is the goal merely to collect ideas for a creative pool or is the task to develop a concrete proposal? Should the developed result be in the form of a to-do list, an action statement or a project report? And how detailed should the workshop result be recorded at all? Only your client has the answers to these questions, and you should clarify all open questions with them in advance during a meeting. This is also an opportunity to ask about his general motives for the workshop. Does he intend to motivate his employees, to shake them up or to sensitize them to a certain topic? The client's answers will guide the further planning and the concrete course of your workshop. Once the goal has been agreed with the client and clearly defined, it is advisable to formulate it in one or two clearly understandable sentences. In this way, you will not lose sight of your goal at any time. It can also make sense to include the objective in the invitation to the workshop. In this way, you offer the participants sufficient opportunity to think about the task and objective in advance. It is in the nature of a workshop that the results cannot be planned in advance. They only emerge during the course of the work in the groups. Your task as a moderator, on the other hand, is to think in advance about how you want to record the results. After all, they serve as a basis for later planning steps. Once you have agreed on the goals and general conditions with the client, you can start inviting your workshop participants. For reasons of planning, this should definitely be done in good time. If you think it makes sense, you can add a description of how to get there or information about a desired dress code to the invitation. When invitations are sent out, all participants with special duties are also informed of their duties. These may be guest speakers or selected employees who are to work on a specific task in advance, with the aim of enabling a smooth transition into the workshop work.

Sensible composition of the participants

If you are completely unfamiliar with the participants of your workshop, only a consultative discussion with your client can provide orientation. He will be best able to assess in which group constellation constructive results can be achieved. When planning, make sure that the composition of the group is as heterogeneous as possible. Different hierarchies, age groups, interests, experiences and genders guarantee different views, opinions and perspectives. These are good prerequisites for filling the objectives, which are still very formal at the beginning of the workshop, with creative content as the workshop progresses. Selectively invite people who are in a position to make valuable contributions to the outcome. If your participants have the appropriate expertise, this will undoubtedly be reflected in the quality of the results. You should also make sure that enough participants with decision-making authority are invited. Is your workshop designed to produce concrete results that will later be implemented? Then remember to invite the people who will be responsible for implementing the results after the workshop. In this way, you won't leave anyone out, you won't step on anyone's toes, and you will thus ensure the practical implementation of the results. The number of participants will also have a decisive influence on the design of your workshop. Because it decides on possible group formations and methods that can be used. In general, it can be said that a number of participants of up to 15 can be coordinated very well by a moderator alone. However, if the number of participants is higher, you should consider the support of another moderator.

Sensible structures for your workshop

Workshops usually last half a day to two days. It is essential that you think about a sensible structure before the start of the workshop. A rough schedule will facilitate your planning and ensure that you don't lose sight of the timetable you have set. For example, dividing a workshop day into four blocks can be a perfectly sensible procedure. If each block lasts about 90 minutes and two blocks take place in the morning and two in the afternoon, you will have established a rough timetable which, with sufficient break times, corresponds to a working day of eight hours. Based on such a schedule, appropriate focal points and suitable methods can then be assigned to each block. Now that you have the rough schedule of your workshop, you can start answering the following questions. How do you want to open the workshop and in what way should the topic be presented to the participants? In which order should the given topics be dealt with? How much time is available for each topic? Which rules are important to you? Which moderation techniques do you prefer and how do you skillfully accommodate them in the workshop? How do you intend to handle the use of technical equipment? At which points are breaks useful? How would you like to end the workshop? You should allow more time for complex topics, because explanations, assistance and questions from participants require sufficient space. Concentrated work also requires sufficient break times; they allow your participants to clear their heads and stretch their legs. Answering all these questions will result in a kind of script that outlines the flow of your workshop. Once your personal flow is in place, you can start rehearsing your facilitation. Don't hesitate to ask colleagues, relatives and friends for their opinion, because every feedback can bring you a bit closer to your goal: professional facilitation of a successful workshop.

Suitable premises and catering

Before conducting your workshop, clarification of the following points is an absolute prerequisite: You need a sufficiently large venue with a suitable ambience and room equipment that offers sufficient retreat options for planned group work. In addition, this venue must have an adequate infrastructure that ensures the use of all the materials you require and guarantees the provision of catering. For the latter point, the duration of your workshop is decisive. For example, a workshop lasting several hours certainly does not require an elaborate meal, but the organization of small snacks, water or coffee is still one of your tasks. For all-day workshops, participants should be given the opportunity to have lunch. In this case, you should make sure during the planning phase whether the offer already includes the possibility of booking an on-site catering service. If this is not the case, a restaurant in the vicinity is recommended. Find out in advance about opening hours, closing days, kitchen times, capacities and reservation modalities. An alternative is to hire an external provider, whom you will then have to commission with the catering accordingly. Depending on the planning, the choice of premises will be determined on the one hand by the number of participants, and on the other hand by the structure of your workshop. If you are planning to work in small groups, renting several meeting rooms is a good idea. If, on the other hand, you are planning a workshop with the entire group, a correspondingly large room would be the more sensible alternative.

Required material and adequate equipment

On the basis of a well thought-out plan, you can now focus your attention specifically on whether all the tools are available on site to ensure the smooth running of your workshop. For example, do you need a projector or other technical equipment? Do you need flipcharts, index cards, clipboards, Post-Its, pens, scissors or handouts to help you communicate and visualize important information in writing? Do you consider wearing name badges useful and have you remembered to have them made in a timely manner? Questions of this kind will be answered in advance in the course of targeted preparation, so that all equipment and materials are available when the workshop begins. A comprehensive materials list will reliably support you in this and will also make your work easier in the future when planning further workshops. Don't forget: Check all the technical equipment you need in advance to make sure it works and is in good working order, and always have spare batteries for remote controls. This will help you avoid wasting valuable workshop time senselessly due to unwanted interruptions.

Suitable workshop methods

The design of your workshop has a direct influence on its course and the quality of the results achieved. If your workshop is unstructured and boring right from the start, you cannot hope for highly motivated participants. If, on the other hand, you have already dealt with the question in advance, prepared handouts, created meaningful graphics and thought about suitable methods, this will make the path to your goal much easier. For example, a classic method such as mind mapping can support you in organizing the ideas developed in the group and visualizing connections for all to see. This is where the competent moderator shows himself, who knows how to support the participants competently by choosing an appropriate method, without having to step into the foreground himself. The general rule is that one to three different methods can be used, depending on the duration of the workshop. At this point, reference should be made to the third and fourth chapters of this guidebook, in which a wide variety of facilitation methods are described in detail. Just like the design of your workshop, the appropriate methods depend on the topic, goal and number of participants. For example, the Six Thinking Hats are designed only for groups of up to a maximum of 20 participants, while the 2, 4, 8 Consensus can take up to three hours. In addition, the decision to use a method depends heavily on what time of day it is to be used. The early morning calls for different methods than the afternoon, when an exhausting workshop day is already drawing to a close after many discussions. There is always the question of whether the planned method is suitable for the participants. Is it practicable? Are the participants willing to go along? If not, the participants may not take your method seriously, feel uncomfortable and, in the worst case, drop out completely. If this happens, a well-prepared Plan B will know how to prevent the worst.

What events can jeopardize the success of your workshop?

To answer this question, your client should be your first point of contact. He or she will be able to give you valuable advice. Use them specifically to identify potential risks in advance. In this way, you are prepared for all scenarios and can avoid problematic situations or deal with them professionally. In this way, you are well prepared for difficult participants or constellations with conflict potential. A fact that gives both you and the participants of your workshop a reassuring feeling of security. A Plan B also lets you react more calmly in difficult situations. Because then time problems, personal conflicts or blockade attitudes will not throw you off track.

Conclusion: There are many small steps that should be taken one after the other and in a well-considered way in order to lead a workshop to success. During preparation, each of these steps must be well thought out and supplemented with organizational and content-related aspects. If you invest sufficient time here in advance, nothing will stand in the way of the success of your workshop. Do you even have a contingency plan up your sleeve for unforeseen or difficult situations? Perfect, because a successful workshop stands and falls with its preparation.

Preparing for the requirements of different types of workshops

Since a workshop is always conducted in a goal-oriented manner, attention should already be paid to the group constellation, the topic and the objective during the planning phase. During the preparation phase, it is of central importance whether there is a concrete problem within a group, a conflict between two parties, a new concept is to be developed or a decision is to be made. The approach of the moderator must then be adapted to the respective objectives. Is there a problem to be solved, a decision to be made, or is cohesion within the group to be strengthened? These are important questions that require different approaches and can only lead to successful solutions if the principles of the different types of workshops, with all their distinguishing features, are taken into account during the moderation. Because moderation does not happen incidentally, but contributes significantly to success. In order to be able to ensure targeted preparation, the various types of workshops will be briefly classified at this point.

Problem-solving workshops

As the name suggests, problem-solving workshops deal with solving a specific problem. In this case, the workshop proves to be a deliberate instrument used in response to a specific problem that has already arisen within a group. In the first step, the facilitator will be faced with the task of defining the problem in order to then deal with the influencing factors and develop strategies for solving the problem together with the participants. All steps must always be concretely defined, evaluated and presented. The goal of a problem-solving workshop is a consensus supported by all participants, recorded in writing in the form of a catalog of measures. This is a task that requires a great deal of neutrality, knowledge of human nature, organizational talent and empathy in dealing with delicate situations.

Team development workshops/conflict resolution workshops

Our modern working day is subject to constant changes, its structures are becoming more and more complex. In professional interaction, situations can unintentionally arise that lead to problems and conflicts within a team. Resolving these usually requires a neutral mediator, a moderator. In such a complex situation, his or her task is to turn those affected into participants and to actively involve them in the decision-making processes and in finding solutions. This is a real challenge that can only be mastered through foresighted preparation. Team development workshops take two different approaches. As a rule, the members of a newly formed team are facing each other for the first time, possibly a change of leadership, a takeover or a merger has taken place. The primary goal of the workshop is to get to know each other and to get to know each other. If the participants already know each other, the clearly defined goals are improved cooperation on the one hand and the development of team affiliation and team spirit on the other. Tasks that require a lot of knowledge of human nature, empathy and creativity on the part of the person who accompanies the participants through the individual steps on the way to the goal: You! An approach can succeed particularly well in the context of a team development workshop. This is because, away from the normal work routine, an informal environment allows sufficient freedom to approach each other and to get to know each other (better). Here, facilitation is to be understood as a process that adapts individually and methodically to the requirements of the group and, through case-related and solution-oriented work, leads to the emergence of a collaborative team from many individuals. A team that later, in the routine of everyday work, is ready to take responsibility, invest energy, tackle problems together and achieve goals together. A workshop can also be a very useful option for interpersonal problems, especially when conflicts that have arisen in the course of everyday work can no longer be resolved without outside help. In this case, the moderator must be aware of his or her responsibility, since he or she is acting as a mediator between parties whose relationship to each other is already heavily burdened by conflicts, resistance and entrenched positions. Such a conflict resolution workshop must take into account the perspective of all participants, diagnose the causes very sensitively, make suitable offers and combine the wishes of all as satisfactorily as possible. On the way to implementing a catalog of measures, a great deal of negotiating skill and empathy is expected of you as the moderator. Especially here, without adequate preparation and sufficient expertise, finding a solution will hardly be possible, especially since there is a risk that existing conflicts will break out further or, in the worst case, even escalate completely.

Concept workshops/strategy workshops

A conception workshop presents the moderator with completely different challenges. First of all, under his or her guidance, the field of activity is defined, the conceptual goals are clarified and suitable content is developed. For example, the beginning of such a workshop may consist merely of a large, blank sheet of paper, which is filled with creative ideas step by step during the development process. In the plenum, corresponding ideas are evaluated, condensed and passed on. In this way, the participants have enough space to shape a new concept exactly according to their own ideas. On the other hand, it can make perfect sense to present the participants with a conceptual shell that has already been prepared and that only needs to be supplemented and revised by the participants in the further course of the workshop. This is a good option, which has its advantages especially when the time available is relatively limited and quick solutions have to be found. Problems can arise, however, if participants find fault with the guidance provided or feel too restricted in their creative freedom. This quickly creates room for dissatisfaction and, in extreme cases, for questioning the concept offered. Because by presenting a prepared shell, you as the moderator put yourself very much in the foreground, become vulnerable and possibly even get into the unpleasant situation of having to defend yourself. A circumstance that should be avoided at all costs.

Decision-making workshop

Since it is in the nature of a decision workshop to make decisions, the primary task of the facilitator will be to guide the participants to select the most appropriate model from a variety of models. In this respect, the goal is relatively clearly defined here, as alternatives must be presented, evaluation criteria must first be developed and then evaluated in the next step. In the course of such an evaluation phase, models are excluded and at the same time favorites are chosen, of which only one will remain at the end. After the decision has been made, the moderator records the further course of action and corresponding follow-up measures in writing in the catalog of measures. Product workshop/workshop for new product ideas In the course of a product workshop, the focus is on ideas and measures for developing a new product. Necessary measures for adapting an existing product to the changed requirements of the market are also discussed here. Within the workshop, the participants are specifically included in the development process in order to actively participate in the development of creative ideas. Under the professional guidance of a moderator, not only new perspectives but also concrete insights for positioning on the market can emerge.

Criteria for the success of a workshop

A workshop basically takes place outside of the daily work routine. Away from the daily work routine, selected employees gather to work together on the solution of a clearly defined task within a specified time frame. This requires a working atmosphere in which creative potential can unfold freely, because a workshop thrives on the rich pool of ideas of its participants. The team is accompanied on its way by an experienced moderator, who gives structure to the workshop and offers assistance in mastering the tasks. Even if the moderator sets the time structure, care must be taken during planning to leave enough room for flexibility. This is because new ideas and productive work can lead to unexpected changes in the schedule, to which you as the moderator can then react accordingly without creating time pressure. The objective of a workshop is also clearly defined. The participants themselves actively participate in the solution of the problem and are thus prepared to bring about changes, to bear them and to integrate them into their daily work in the future. It is therefore absolutely mandatory for the moderator to follow up on the results and follow up on the implementation.

Chapter 3: Successfully develop strategies and solutions in 5 steps.

Chapter 3.1: Getting started - welcome - occasion - goals - time frame and rules for the event

Even before your guests arrive

In good time before the invited participants arrive for the workshop, you have already prepared everything necessary. In particular, you should use this lead time to check all the aids and electronic equipment that will be used for completeness and functionality. Have you planned drinks or snacks? Then now is the right time to provide them in an appealing way. Can your guests find the premises easily? If not, it is advisable to hang up appropriate notices. Also, have all the necessary materials ready to hand and mentally go through the planned course of your workshop step by step. In this way, you will feel secure, your workshop can begin in a relaxed manner, and you can now devote your full attention to the arriving participants and welcome them in a pleasant working atmosphere. Before your guests arrive, also think about preparing the meeting room, especially the planned seating arrangement. You have already thought about this during the planning stage and adapted the chosen arrangement form accordingly to the number of participants, room size and method. The right seating arrangement will contribute significantly to the success of your workshop, but there are important points to keep in mind. Rows of chairs must allow sufficient legroom and legal regulations must be observed: For example, escape routes must always remain clear and free access to fire extinguishers must be guaranteed at all times. Further, the question arises whether all participants have a good view of you as the moderator from their seats and whether, when using technology, the screens are clearly visible to all.

You will find a detailed overview of suitable seating types for your workshop, together with the respective advantages and disadvantages, at the end of this chapter.

Getting started

At the beginning, participants should first be given enough time to arrive calmly, get to know each other, and begin in a relaxed manner. After all, as individual as the participants of your workshop are, their ideas, wishes and expectations of the workshop are likely to be just as different. Plan enough time for the introduction and, if possible, welcome each participant personally with a handshake. In this way, you lay a solid foundation for a later imaginative collaboration. In this context, entries in a "guest book" that is visible to all guests can also be a good way to provide information about the names, professions, positions or current projects of the participants. For this purpose, you have attached a sufficiently large table to a bulletin board, in which the participants can sign as soon as they arrive at the workshop. In this way, initial contacts are made, faces can be matched more easily, interests become visible, and your guests get into conversation with each other more easily. It is up to your imagination whether you ask things in this context that will cheer up your participants and thus create a positive mood. Perhaps the question of what profession you dreamed of as a child, what item you would take with you to a desert island, or what item you would definitely not take with you.

Welcome & timeline

After all guests are seated, you now officially open your workshop. The actual facilitation situation in front of the group begins. First, it is important that you briefly introduce yourself (again) and welcome the participants to your workshop once more. If the participants do not know each other, a short round of introductions is recommended at this point. Then provide your guests with detailed information about the planned schedule, the time frame and the planned break times. In order to ensure sufficient transparency, it is advisable to list all program points with a concrete schedule on one DIN A4 page. In this way, your guests will always have an overview of the planned schedule and break times, while you can refer to it again and again during the course of the workshop if necessary. A notice board visible to all will have the same effect. You will now benefit from your good preparation when carrying out the defined program points. Because each individual program point stands, including all necessary components and prepared material. This enables you to explain to your participants at each point what is coming up and what is required of them. During the individual work phases you can move from group to group, discreetly assist and specifically answer questions that arise. You will discuss results and solutions together, reflect on their implementation, and in this way create a pleasant working atmosphere in which the participants can work in a self-organized and undisturbed manner. However, you should also always bear in mind that your moderation script only contains a sequence of contents and methods planned in advance in theory. This should provide security as an orientation guide, but should never be so rigidly defined that it no longer allows for flexible deviations. If you reach the point where your script no longer fits the development in the plenum, you should always be able to adapt to new situations, contents and group constellations by means of a Plan B.

Rules for the event

In this phase, the rules that apply to the workshop are also clearly defined. How will cell phones, Blackberries and laptops be handled and what rules of conversation apply? In this way, you create a pleasant working atmosphere right from the start and thus the ideal basis for effective work and thus for the success of your workshop. Clarify together with the group that certain rules apply within your workshop that must be observed and that you will intervene if they are not observed. For example, one of the most important rules will certainly be that participants let each other finish and do not interrupt each other. This is the only way to create a constructive discussion at eye level that is characterized by mutual respect and in which each participant can develop the good feeling of being taken seriously and being listened to sufficiently. At this point, you as the moderator can also specifically ask the group whether it makes sense and is desirable to limit the speaking time per contribution. If this is the case, your task in the further course will be to ensure that the agreed speaking time is adhered to. A respectful discussion culture also includes tolerating the opinions of others. After all, differing opinions and points of view are the driving force within a workshop that makes it possible to develop a common approach to a solution. Make your participants aware that differing views should not automatically be interpreted as personal attacks and that you want a working atmosphere that is characterized by tolerance towards other views and in dealing with each other. A working atmosphere in which no other discussion partner is badmouthed or embarrassed, but which is rather characterized by objectivity, fairness and acceptance. Discussions thrive on the fact that different views come together. So if understandable objections or justified criticism are voiced, you as the moderator should keep a close eye on the situation and - if necessary - point out that both objections and criticism serve to work together to improve the circumstances. After all, without the existence of problems, this workshop would not have happened in the first place. Should a discussion get completely out of hand and the participants start arguing with each other, it is your task to calm down the heated tempers again. This guidebook offers you practical assistance in dealing with difficult situations in Chapter 5. To avoid interrupting constructive work processes and discussions with loud ringing, annoying message tones and/or vibrating notifications, define another important rule at this point: cell phones, Blackberries, laptops, etc. off! But be careful! Do not overload your participants with a flood of rules. Three to four rules that are relevant to you are absolutely sufficient at the beginning. Otherwise, you could easily get the impression that your regulatory frenzy is intended to patronize the participants. This is not a good starting position for creative cooperation. And in this context, always remember that no matter what rule you set up, you as the moderator are responsible for adhering to it. If necessary, it is your task to first make eye contact, address the troublemaker by name and then remind him or her in a friendly but firm manner to observe the rule.

Occasion & goals of the workshop

Now it is time to define the actual purpose of the workshop and prepare the participants for what the workshop is about. You explain what specific goal is being pursued and in what way and by what means you intend to achieve this goal. The clearer you do this, the better participants will know why they are here and what is expected of them. By defining a main goal, you steer your participants' idea potential in the right direction right from the start. Ideally, they will generate a variety of creative ideas and approaches to solutions without getting lost in side issues. And, of course, participants are also given ample opportunity to express their expectations of the workshop. Listen carefully here and always keep an eye on the comments made.

Your goal for this phase of facilitation

The primary goal of this first phase of your facilitation will be to ensure that all participants have arrived at your workshop both physically and mentally. The more positive you make the opening of your workshop, the more pleasant the basic mood, working atmosphere and joint cooperation will be in the further course. Since every workshop is subject to a certain sequence, all participants are now informed about the time schedule that applies to this workshop. If the participants are clearly informed by you as the moderator about the framework conditions, rules, working methods and objectives from the very beginning, security is created and possible misunderstandings can be ruled out from the outset. The decision as to how the opening of your workshop should proceed methodically is yours alone. Whether you decide on a purely verbal opening or give preference to a more elaborate orientation flipchart depends on your personal taste and, of course, on the respective circumstances. Inspirations and practical suggestions for this phase of the workshop.

About rounds of introductions that no one finds uncomfortable

Rounds of introductions should absolutely be taken with a grain of salt. The generic request - "Why don't you tell us about yourself ..." - can end in minutes-long monologues as well as in reluctantly uttered short sentences. Not everyone likes to divulge key data from their own life, especially not when twelve pairs of strangers' eyes are directed at them. For this reason, methods that keep individual information to a minimum can be useful. For example, you can ask participants to introduce themselves in just two sentences. The first sentence should contain their name, the second the reason for their presence in your workshop. Done! Games in which two partners interview each other and then present their respective answers to the group are also not to everyone's taste. Introverts find this kind of small talk neither particularly fun nor particularly loosening. Therefore, you should only use methods that you, as the moderator, are fully convinced of yourself. Methods that may already have proven themselves in practice. However, if it is important to you as a moderator to learn something about the current mood or about certain preferences of your participants, you can easily extend the minimum by this information. A very pleasant method for this is the so-called "personal object". The group (maximum 20 people) sits in a circle, with a blank sheet of paper in the middle. Now everyone is supposed to take an object out of their pocket that is of special importance to them. This object is placed on the sheet, outlined with a pencil and put back into the bag. One by one, each participant can now choose an outline and the owner of the corresponding object can explain for what reason this object is personally important to him. Thus, this method has the advantage that everyone can tell something about themselves, but decides for themselves what and how much they want to reveal about themselves. The so-called flash method inquires about expectations and feelings. Participants respond spontaneously to your question in words or short sentences. Otherwise, only two rules apply to this method: All participants express themselves in the "I" form, comments and statements are not allowed. The "guest book" already mentioned should also be briefly recalled in this context because of its many advantages.

About sensible planning and use of break times.

The duration of your workshop is determined by the client, because it is he who specifies the total time available. It is then your responsibility to structure this time frame and determine a sensible organizational schedule. When planning, you will therefore inevitably have to deal with the question of how many breaks there will be and what length these breaks should be. Based on a one-day workshop, the rule of thumb is that there should be a break after one and a half hours. So when planning your workshop, keep an eye from the outset on ensuring that the individual blocks do not exceed a duration of 90 minutes. As a rough guide, you can plan a time frame of 15 to 30 minutes for the first coffee break. Here, standing tables ensure that your participants keep moving and get to know each other better. As a moderator, you will also be able to make good use of this break, as it provides you with an opportunity for small talk. Don't hesitate to address your participants personally and - if the setting allows it - remember all their names as soon as possible. Your participants will appreciate it if you, as the moderator, know the names from memory as you go along and don't have to keep squinting awkwardly at the name tags. In addition, learning the names quickly demonstrates appreciation and allows for polite and respectful interaction. Plan for a full hour for lunch and another coffee break of 15 to 30 minutes after the third block in the early afternoon. In the case of workshops lasting several days, you will ideally even receive valuable information in break situations that can be very useful in the further course. Note down statements of this kind immediately and also note which participant this information came from. If you now memorize them overnight, you can use all the information very specifically to your advantage in the next few days.

About choosing the right form of seating

The type of seating you choose depends on numerous factors. For example, the spatial conditions and the size of the expected number of participants will have a significant influence on your decision. The type of seating you choose should create a pleasant working atmosphere and give everyone a clear view of you as the presenter. Depending on how you plan to structure your workshop, you will either choose seating that encourages discussion among each other or seating that focuses forward. Planned group work can then be moved out to seminar rooms. If you are still unsure about the appropriate form, suitable software may be able to help you make the right choice. It takes over planning and calculation and calculates in detail and to scale the required number of chairs and tables based on the available space. After all, different seating arrangements require different amounts of space - and with identical numbers of people! A simple chair circle does without tables and therefore offers decisive advantages. It is the most communicative type of seating, since all participants can see each other well and are invited to a lively exchange of ideas. For this reason, the chair circle is particularly suitable for workshops that are geared towards active togetherness, interaction and discussion rounds. The decisive disadvantage of the chair circle is that, due to the absence of tables, there is no workplace. The same applies to the so-called theater seating, in which the chairs are placed one behind the other - usually staggered - in rows. It is considered a suitable form of seating for workshops with large rooms and high numbers of participants and allows everyone a good view to the front. As with the circle of chairs, the disadvantage is the lack of a table; in addition, discussions can only take place with difficulty, the participants take on a rather passive role and have relatively little space available. For this reason, the distance between the back of the chair and the beginning of the next chair should be between 60 and 70 centimeters. If tables arranged in parallel rows are added, this form of seating strongly resembles that of a classroom. With the so-called parliamentary seating arrangement, the use of working materials and the taking of notes are possible without any problems. However, you need correspondingly more space due to the use of tables. The available space is used less optimally, and conversations and discussions are made more difficult because the participants sit one behind the other. The block table or block seating is considered modern and contemporary and can be quickly and variably adapted to the given conditions. It is ideal for workshops where a lot of space is needed to work. Chairs are arranged around one or more usually rectangular table blocks with the advantage that presenter and participants can see each other very well and communicate directly. Usually up to 14 people sit at one table, none of the seating positions are exposed. Even if several seminar tables are used, there are always good passageways for you as the moderator, so that all tables and all participants can be reached at any time without any problems.

However, it is important to remember that with this type of seating, there will always be participants who sit with their backs to you and have to turn around to follow what you are saying. Thus, the block table is more designed for workshops whose focus is primarily on interaction. The carré shape is similar to the block table except that it leaves an area in the middle free for good visibility, communication and comfortable legroom. The carré shape is particularly suitable for workshops on a larger scale. Its disadvantage is that it requires large premises due to its high space requirements. If there is such a thing as the ideal seating shape for workshops, the U-shape will certainly occupy one of the top spots. As the name suggests, the tables are placed in a U-shape and surrounded by chairs only on the outer sides. The interior will remain completely free. Since the U-shape results in an open side, the presenter has an interesting opportunity to use the entire interior space for his purposes and actively interact with the participants. In the midst of his guests, the presenter can move freely, communicate and distribute important documents at the same time. For the participants, this form of seating offers a good view to the front, eye contact with each other, conversations at eye level, comfortable legroom and still enough space to work. The longer you make the U-sides, the more people you can seat. Note, however, that mutual eye contact may then become more difficult, because the U-shape is only suitable for smaller groups of up to 20 people. The so-called E-shape results from the arrangement of the seminar tables in the shape of an "E". All tables are surrounded by chairs. This seating arrangement has a decisive advantage for your workshop: It offers enough space for many participants in small seminar rooms. In addition, a direct counterpart and direct eye contact invite an informal exchange of ideas. These are ideal conditions for your workshop, especially since the tables offer sufficient space for storing work materials. One disadvantage of the E-shape is the close proximity of the participants. This means that you may not be able to reach individual participants as easily as you would with a block table or U-shape. In this case, the number of participants, room size and methods must be weighed up. The herringbone shape offers several advantages to you as a presenter. By arranging the tables at an angle towards the workshop leader's desk, all participants have an equally good view of the flipchart, pin board or projection screen. The opportunity for interaction between you and the participants proves ideal. The chairs are located behind the tables, the view to the front is not disturbed by anything - enough space to work and legroom included. Since the herringbone shape focuses forward, the disadvantage is that discussions among participants are made more difficult. The constant turning of the head in the direction of the moderator can also be perceived as unpleasant in the long term. In addition, this form of seating is extremely space-intensive.

Chapter 3.2: Determining the initial situation - collecting and structuring information

Determining the starting position

If the objectives are now clear, the actual work can begin. However, it will not be possible to start the creative process until the "as-is" situation is clearly defined, when all participants are aware of the current state of the problem. Here, short presentations, topic-oriented discussions or short speeches by those affected can be suitable means of bringing all participants up to the same level of knowledge. The audience should neither be bombarded with too much technical knowledge nor be overwhelmed with too much information. A minimum of uniform information is sufficient to enable each participant in the workshop to contribute and actively participate in finding a solution. If all participants now have a clear idea of the starting position, the creative part of the workshop - the generation of ideas and measures - can begin. When selecting topics for the agenda, all participants should be involved on an equal footing. After all, those who actively participate in proposing important topics leave the passive position of the affected party and move into the active role of the participant. This creates room for a sense of community, participants feel they are being taken seriously, and resulting outcomes are later shared.

Gathering and structuring information

The way in which you access the creative ideas of your participants has already been thoroughly considered when planning your workshop. It is entirely up to you to decide whether you prefer to use the questionnaire or the card questionnaire at this point. Both techniques belong to the standard repertoire of every professional moderator and will therefore be examined in more detail below. However, in order to offer you a broader choice of methods, the fourth chapter of this guide presents five other creative techniques. You should give preference to the method that appeals to you the most and can be implemented most effectively in practice. Only when you know how to handle your method with confidence can innovative ideas emerge and goal-oriented problem-solving strategies be developed.

The shout-out question (brainstorming)

The shout-out question is always used where creative thinking is to be promoted and many ideas are to be collected. This method is introduced by you as the moderator by clearly stating the topic. Then you ask the participants to shout out all ideas on this topic spontaneously and loudly, without censorship, without thinking - even crazy ideas are explicitly welcome! Discussions, evaluations or critical comments, on the other hand, are expressly unwanted. Ideas that have already been mentioned may be taken up and further developed at any time and with pleasure, because the shout-out query does not provide for copyright protection or copyright. With the beginning of the creative phase you will certainly need support. For this reason, appoint one or two helpers whose task it will be to write down the collected ideas in half sentences for all to see. In this way, you will generate a large number of good approaches that will later serve as the basis for further work in the workshop. As a time orientation for the shout-out, a variable duration between five and 30 minutes is suggested. The disadvantage of the shout-out question is that you as the moderator will have to deal with many different problems. The shout-out question requires your participants to think very quickly, to follow along with concentration, and to have the courage to suggest topics in plenary. On the other hand, this is countered by group dynamic processes. Not every participant is extroverted, wants to speak up in front of others and has an assertive personality. Participants who combine these traits are therefore at a clear advantage over the others. This is a severe disadvantage when looking for a creative technique that wants to use the full potential of the group. Another disadvantage of the shout-out is the simultaneous logging of the many creative ideas, which you as the facilitator cannot handle alone. The role of the facilitator in this method of idea generation requires mastering several tasks. For example, he or she must motivate the group with his or her suggestions, slow down overzealous participants, support reticent ones, and at the same time make sure that everyone in the group is sufficiently heard. As a moderator, you should always keep an eye on the fact that the brainstorming remains goal-oriented and does not get lost in unimportant details and sprawling discussions. You must never take sides and must maintain an overview of the overall development at all times. This is because one of your tasks at the end of the meeting will be to prepare a protocol that must reflect all the ideas collected in an orderly fashion. Reason enough to refer at this point to a method that makes use of all the advantages of the shout-out questioning, but at the same time knows how to skilfully circumnavigate the disadvantages of this method: the Metaplan technique.

The Metaplan Technique

The Metaplan technique can be used wherever the focus is on promoting creative and open-ended processes. During the brainstorming phase, this facilitation technique can help you collect and structure the many different - perhaps completely incompatible - ideas and visualize them for all to see. This method is particularly well suited for workshops because each participant can individually, actively and independently contribute to finding a solution. This is a decisive advantage, because in this way all competencies of the group can be used in a result-oriented way. For this technique, you will preferably use a freely positionable pin board to attach all topics, ideas and suggestions to. Wrapping paper (1.5 × 1.25 meters) is used as a support for the moderation cards, which is attached to the pinboard beforehand. Other equipment includes moderation cards in various sizes, colors and shapes, pins, different colored felt-tip pens of various widths, glue sticks and small adhesive dots in different colors. Digital camera or cell phone are ideal for creating a photo protocol. Completely equipped moderation cases are available in stores. As a moderator, you play a particularly important role in the Metaplan technique, because your moderation is crucial to its success. A lot is demanded from you in the professional handling of the Metaplan technique. You have to take on the role of a neutral mediator, not only structuring all steps and results, but also visualizing them in a suitable form. In doing so, you must always remain in the background and under no circumstances influence results or possible solutions, let alone prescribe them. Even though this method is said to be somewhat antiquated, it has lost none of its activating potential.

The card query technique (brainwriting)

You preferably start the creative idea search by clearly posting the goal, which is already clearly defined at this point, on the bulletin board. Handing out cards and thick felt-tip pens to the participants, you now start collecting creative suggestions and ideas. Even before the search for ideas begins, ask participants to write on the cards only in keywords, in large letters, and legibly. Due to their self-adhesive properties, larger-format Post-its can be a useful alternative to moderation cards, pins or glue. Each participant writes down his or her own individual thoughts, goes to the wall and hangs his or her labeled cards in any free space. An alternative to this would be for you, as the facilitator, to take over this task, collect the finished cards and, as they are hung up, already read out the card contents. If you realize during this section that there are too many cards, ask the participants to make a pre-selection. The decision about which card is important or less important is left to the participant alone. If you, as the moderator, immediately visualize the collected arguments during this phase, a structured working basis has already been created. Your visualization offers the great advantage that each participant can follow the arguments of the others and knows from which point of view they view the topic. You can graphically highlight irreconcilable points of view in a simple way, for example, in the form of lightning bolts. Now hang all the ideas, pick out related topics and arrange ("cluster") them in thematically appropriate groups. In this phase, it is extremely important to always align your thoughts with the participants and to actively involve them in the process of sorting. To achieve this, discuss the individual ideas with the participants and at the same time clarify the content of unclearly formulated keywords. In doing so, do not explicitly look for the author, but rather involve the entire plenary with the question of what could be meant here. Multiple ideas are simply piled on top of each other, while non-clusterable ideas initially find a place on the side. A great deal of sensitivity is required of the moderator at this stage, because sensitive participants will always take criticism of any kind personally.

All the more reason for the idea evaluation to be in the hands of a trained moderator, whose skillful moderation makes the idea generation phase clear and motivating for everyone. Afterwards, interact with the participants to find suitable headings, discuss them and attach them to the appropriate topic group. When the last heading is attached, the process of "clustering" is finished and the result, which is visible to all, can be used as a basis for the further development of your workshop. Even in this so important phase, never forget that you yourself always act only as a neutral outsider. Once the agenda topics have been identified and visualized, the next question is how to prioritize them. Where should the focus be? Where could success be achieved most quickly? In what order should the main topics be worked on? Together, the group votes on which topics should be worked on as a matter of priority. Here, too, the collaborative idea is in the foreground; in this way, endless discussions are avoided from the outset and the remaining time can be effectively filled with meaningful content. A popular evaluation method is the so-called multivoting. It is relatively easy to use, avoids unnecessary discussions, is democratic and at the same time identifies the most important ideas. Equipped with sticky dots, the participants become active in this method. The number of available sticky dots depends on the number of alternatives available, but should not exceed two-thirds of all possibilities. Together, everyone now comes forward for evaluation and asks themselves which topics are of greater relevance. Preferred ideas receive points accordingly; it was agreed in advance whether only one point or several points may be allocated to an idea. Once all points have been allocated, a jointly developed result is spread out before everyone's eyes: A list sorted by importance of the topics, which is supported by all and whose further treatment now nothing more stands in the way. As the moderator, you will take this list home with you or photograph it and record all the ideas and focal points so that you can send them to all the participants in written form after the workshop.

About advantages and problems of the Metaplan technique

If you moderate a workshop in which the participants do not know each other, the creative exchange of ideas begins immediately with the generation of ideas. Filling in, attaching and evaluating the content invites lively discussions and activity, no participant is left out and a first approach can take place completely casually. The Metaplan technique makes it possible to generate a large number of creative ideas, because it knows how to use the full potential of all the participants present. Due to the anonymous character, the generation of ideas is not restricted. Ideally, completely crazy ideas emerge that open up new perspectives and would perhaps never have come to light in a different setting. Once all the main topics have been visualized and evaluated, the participants are satisfied with the result of the work they have done together, without endless discussions having previously tired the participants rather than generating fruitful ideas. At this point it should be mentioned that the Metaplan technique is only designed for a group size of eight to 15 people. However, the Metaplan technique also poses problems. Despite all the advice, there will be participants who produce poorly readable maps. For example, the font may be too small, unreadable, or more than one idea on the card. When clarifying content, always be careful not to snub the participant in any way. Another problem could arise from clustering disagreements that can end up in unnecessary and time-consuming discussions. This is where you should step in and end the discussion. Another disadvantage of the Metaplan technique is that voting by sticky dots is neither free nor secret. If everyone can see what the other person's opinion is, the decision may not be a free one. In addition, participants can significantly influence decisions using this method by selectively sticking dots.

Chapter 3.3: Addressing and discussing different topics and developing solutions together.

At this point, a methodologically trained facilitator should be faced with a satisfied and motivated group that is willing to continue to actively participate. A point of crucial importance, since in the next step - the core phase of your workshop - decisions must be made and problems solved together. During this phase of work, the previously decided topics are often dealt with in small groups, in which selected topics are worked on in a self-organized manner. Working in small groups combines several advantages. In a smaller setting, each participant has sufficient time and opportunity to express him or herself. Even reserved individuals feel less intimidated and are more willing to share their opinions on a topic. Compared to large groups, a dynamic exchange of ideas can take place here, as many actively participate in solving a task. This makes working in small groups extremely efficient, especially from the point of view that several topics can be dealt with at the same time. In order to benefit from this efficiency, the task must first be clearly defined by you as the moderator. It is advisable to write these clearly visible on flipchart paper. Refer to time constraints and remind the group that the results developed must later be presented to the entire group. During the work process, you only intervene as needed, encourage the exchange of ideas among the group members, and never lose sight of the common thread. Ultimately, the method you select in advance will determine the course of this productive core phase. After all, you have already thought in detail about whether the work at this point of the workshop should take place in small groups or in plenary. Professional visualization also ensures maximum transparency during the actual work phase. This can be done using a flip chart, pin board, overhead projector, laptop or beamer. If meeting topics, interim results and outcomes are recorded directly and visibly for everyone, you ensure that the participants continue to pay attention to you and that all the steps and solutions worked out remain comprehensible for each participant. In this way, the progress of the work process becomes visible step by step and can be used as a reference source at any time. In addition, you motivate your participants through a public visualization of the progress and work results that is visible to all, but on the other hand you also draw attention to points where there is still a need for action or clarification. In this way, you achieve the primary goal: working on the previously collected meeting topics according to the respective objective. Through your transparent presentation, misunderstandings can be ruled out from the outset, as all participants actively participate in deciding which content is visualized. A further advantage of this transparency is that the acceptance of the visualized work results is usually very high, since it concerns results compiled independently in the groups. (or: "[...] results worked out in the group are concerned.") This last paragraph makes it very clear that you as a moderator must master the process of visualization. How else are you going to convey the flood of abstract topics, thought processes, and results in a way that everyone can understand? That's why it's important to first learn the basics of visualization and then take the following advice to heart: practice, practice, practice. Now, at this point, it could be assumed that solving problems means the end of the workshop. This is by no means the case, because without targeted planning of the next steps, the results just worked out and solutions found could not be implemented sustainably.

About setting and keeping time limits

Limiting time within a workshop is not only absolutely essential for keeping your pre-established schedule. The so-called Parkinson's Law states that work expands in exactly the same measure as the time available to complete it. This means that at the beginning of a work order, the processing is approached in a more relaxed manner than towards the end, when the deadline is approaching and "panic" slowly rises. It is precisely this phase that is considered to be the most productive and for this reason should be used by you in a targeted manner. Therefore, always keep an eye on the time and always refer directly to the deadline you have set during the work process. The closer you get to the deadline, the more diligently and with greater concentration your participants will work and the better the results you will achieve with your workshop.

What makes a good facilitator at this stage of the workshop?

If you, as a professional moderator, are able to lead your workshop confidently, the participants can easily get the impression that moderation actually looks "quite easy". From their point of view, you talk and ask questions, explain, make suggestions, give the floor, and seemingly incidentally visualize the results and solutions developed by the group. In the process, your guests easily overlook the fact that you, as the moderator, must keep the overall situation and the goal in mind at all times during your moderation. Participants do not perceive that during the moderation process you are constantly consciously asking yourself in which situation you are speaking and in which situation a question is appropriate. They don't realize that you give the floor depending on the situation and that your role as moderator depends heavily on being able to correctly interpret the verbal and nonverbal reactions of your participants. And if your moderation is also characterized by a certain lightness of touch, the participants won't even notice that suggestions on your part are specifically used as food for thought only when the current work process stalls or deviates too much from the objective. So if all the participants envy your easy job, you may have done everything right.

Methods for fatigue and lack of concentration

Your participants have been working diligently and the whiteboard is full of creative ideas, but their concentration is noticeably waning and they are starting to run out of steam. Just such a situation is a good opportunity for a round of exercise, laughter and good humor. Games are very well suited for this, but they are also always a tricky thing. Participants are not always up for it, often feel uncomfortable, embarrassed or paraded in game situations. For this reason, no participant should ever be forced to play. As a moderator, you need extremely fine antennae in order to observe the situation precisely and assess it correctly. If you have the feeling from the start that the group is not ready for a game, a cup of coffee or a few steps in the fresh air are equally effective alternatives. At this point, we will deliberately suggest only four games that have already proven themselves in practice, do not require much effort, avoid unpleasant situations, and are designed to focus on movement and fun. Even if you yourself have doubts and think that perhaps not all participants will enjoy getting physically closer, roaring like tigers or showing claws, you should still give it a try as part of a workshop. Be brave, in this way you will gain practical experience and may even be positively surprised.

The Gordian Knot

This game is designed for ten to 20 participants and belongs to the category of peace games. It is generally popular, easy to implement, and can be played in a wide variety of ways. Allow up to ten minutes for one round. Participants stand in a circle, close their eyes, walk toward each other with arms outstretched, and each tries to grab and hold two hands. In this way, a colorful jumble of knotted arms is created. Now the eyes may be opened again. The aim of the game is to untangle the knot by stepping over and under it in such a way that one (or more) human chains are created. Of course, the hands must not be let go in the process. Instead of a circle, participants can also stand close together and look for hands. People who are obviously uncomfortable with the physical closeness can be outsiders to help the group untangle. If the group and helper are not allowed to talk, the difficulty level increases when the group closes their eyes right away. The Gordian knot promotes group dynamics, because the problem can only be solved through verbal or non-verbal communication. In addition, it promotes the reduction of fear of contact in an entertaining way and provides movement after sitting for a long time. The method is also so well suited for a workshop because untangling the Gordian knot shows that together as a team, you are able to master "tangled" and difficult situations.

Make rain

When heads are smoking from hard work, the game Make Rain provides a welcome "cool down." The game provides mental distraction and creates a calm, pleasant and friendly atmosphere. It takes just five minutes, the number of participants is not limited - a semicircle is enough. This is divided into three groups and you explain that all together will now create an acoustic thunderstorm. Four sounds are needed for this: for drizzle, the palms of the hands are rubbed lightly together, as when washing your hands - for light rain, the hands are rubbed together faster and more audibly in the opposite direction, from top to bottom - for heavy rain, a clap in the hands is planned - for hail, as loud a clap as possible with a hollow hand on the thighs. The goal now will be to let a thunderstorm develop by your guidance, which begins with light drizzle, reaches its climax with strong hail and ends after the thunderstorm in absolute silence. You give the signs in each case, each sound is performed by the group until they receive a new sign from you. So group 1 starts with drizzle, then group 2, then group 3. Now group 1 starts producing light rain, followed by group 2 and group 3. Now it goes on like this in turn until all three groups produce loud hail. Then it goes back through heavy rain, light rain and drizzle until absolute silence returns after the thunderstorm.

Japanese puzzle - old mother, samurai and tiger

In this game, two teams face each other. The basic idea is based on the game scissors, stone, paper, in which three figures can outdo each other. Here, however, an entire team has to agree on a figure together and then compete against the opposing team. In the process, the old mother bends over on her imaginary stick and curses "Dududud" with a raised index finger. In this way she intimidates the samurai and will win this round against him. The samurai, on the other hand, holds his imaginary sword in his hand, lunges forward, shouts loudly "Ha!", thrusts, and thus defeats the tiger. The tiger, in turn, forms his hands into claws, lunges forward, roars fearsomely and "eats" the little old lady without further ado. The game is very simple and has a high fun factor. At the beginning, briefly demonstrate the actions of the characters themselves and also let the group practice the respective movement sequence. Now everyone is ready to go. The team members decide for one of the three figures, you give the command ONE TWO and with THREE all team members change accordingly into old mothers, samurai or tigers. Depending on which figure a team has chosen, they will now win or lose. If both teams choose the same figure, the round is repeated. Five rounds are played, after which the winning team is crowned.

Elephant game

The elephant game provides movement, laughter, fun and good humor. The participants form a circle, one participant stands in the middle, points to any participant and says a certain word - for example: "elephant". This participant now makes an elephant's trunk. The entertaining thing about this game, however, is that both neighbors are also involved in the task. This is because they must now use their arms to form the left and right ears of the elephant. First introduce three variations, then the next three and so on. In this way, the game becomes more and more complex and the entertainment value for everyone increases. There are many variations to choose from for this game. Maybe you have another great idea of your own. How about a kangaroo that indicates a bag with its arms while its neighbors jump up and down? The palm tree takes both arms up, the neighbors only one each - but then they wave together. For the camel cue, the participant in the center bends forward while his two neighbors suggest two humps on their backs. The duck requires a beak indicated with both hands and two supporters who are willing to wiggle their butts. The neighbors are also on the move for the next cue: While the washing machine rubs its belly with one hand, the laundry is flung to the left and right by belly-dancing movements. The whale throws its head into the neck and blows upwards, while swimming movements are performed on both sides. In the cuckoo clock, the participant in the middle calls out "cuckoo" and simultaneously walks with his head forward while the other two perform pendulum movements with their right arms. The toaster is also entertaining, with neighbors holding hands while the finished toast bounces up inside their arms. Those who don't pay attention, don't react fast enough, or make a mistake, have to enter the circle themselves. During the game your participants get other thoughts, have exercise and can continue with their work in a good mood afterwards.

Chapter 3.4: Planning measures and setting deadlines

After collecting ideas, evaluating and discussing them, the next step is to draw up an action plan. Such a plan includes the targeted delegation of task packages. The goal here is usually the creation of a complete to-do list, whose tasks are distributed fairly and according to the participant competencies in consultation with the group. As a professional moderator, you provide targeted support here by visually fixing the results and formulating them as concretely as possible. A table that is visible to all is particularly suitable for this purpose, in which the activities to be completed (What?) with the responsible person (Who?) and time limit (By when?) are recorded in a binding manner. The table should also leave enough space for additional comments. Especially when it comes to the question of who is responsible, you as the moderator are expected to show a great deal of diplomacy, because now your workshop participants have to show their colors and make a binding commitment to complete tasks. Under no circumstances should participants get the feeling that tasks are being shoved at them. On the other hand, more dominant participants should not be given the chance to take over tasks without a common consensus. And what about the participants who do not volunteer for any task? In your role as moderator, you must radiate calm, take into account the competencies of each participant, and maintain an overview at all times. So, at the end of this quite critical phase, when all the results have been documented, those responsible have been named, a target date has been set and a results check has been agreed, your participants and you as the moderator can enter the final phase of the workshop with satisfaction. However, do not forget to record all the results of your action plan after the workshop and to send them to each participant in written form.

Chapter 3.5: Shaping the closing

Now it is time to initiate the closing phase and dismiss the participants. This can be done by a verbal farewell alone, but a summary of the process or a short presentation of the results will round off your workshop. In this way, you ensure a positive conclusion and dismiss your participants with the good feeling of having been productive and having achieved something. This is also an opportunity to reflect on the joint work process. If there is a suitable opportunity, you can ask the participants for constructive feedback. What went well? Could something be done even better? In this way, participants are given the opportunity for maneuver critique. A nice idea to time this feedback is the following: Each participant whose turn it is lights a match and is allowed to talk exactly until it goes out again. You should listen very carefully here, because the criticism expressed in the feedback round - no matter whether it is positive or negative - can serve as inspiration for you and significantly influence the quality of future workshops. If you have the feeling that your workshop did not go well, it is better to refrain from directly asking for feedback at this point. Think about ending your successful workshop in a friendly and relaxed atmosphere? Then how about a closing game? It only takes a few minutes and is called "Workshop Gifts". Each participant receives his or her gift in the form of a card that you have labeled beforehand and explains what kind of gift is on his or her card and what he or she would do with such a gift. What would the participant do with an "invisible magic cloak" or an "airplane that flies him everywhere"? With a "fairy that fulfills three wishes" or with a "lottery ticket that won"? In this way, you can reflect and laugh together once again before your workshop comes to a relaxed conclusion. When all participants have left and silence has returned, you should immediately note down everything that struck you during the course of your moderation. What did you do well and could therefore be used again in the next workshop? What didn't go so well and should be improved next time or possibly avoided altogether? This kind of critical self-reflection enables you to continuously develop your personal skills, which will certainly be reflected in the quality of further workshops in the future. The follow-up of a workshop also includes the creation and sending of minutes, which you should send to the participants as soon as possible. The minutes contain all key results, measures decided upon, lists of activities as well as topics not worked on. It may be useful to include the most important visualizations in the form of photos so that you can still refer to specific details within the work process at a later date. Only now is the work for you as the moderator finished.

Chapter 4: Moderation methods

Effective methods for generating ideas

With the metaplan technique, card questioning and shout-out questioning, common creative techniques have already been explained in detail in Chapter 3. Nevertheless, this guidebook does not want to deprive you of a selection of further possibilities for promoting innovative ideas. As a rule, methods of this kind are designed for groups of between seven and fourteen people and require a time commitment of 30 to 60 minutes. Since the range of possible methods is enormous, only a selection of particularly practicable methods can be mentioned here. Each of them serves to generate initial ideas, which are then evaluated, fleshed out and further developed in the further course of the workshop. As the facilitator, you select the creative technique you think is most appropriate, explain the process, and guide your participants through the entire development process in a supportive manner.

6-3-5 method

This creative technique is ideal when the process of brainstorming needs to be set in motion. Where does the method get its name? Well, six people label their sheets with three ideas each, which are then passed around five times in total. In this way, up to 108 new ideas can be generated within a relatively short period of time of no more than 30 minutes. The 6-3-5 method is particularly constructive because it specifically accesses the previously generated ideas of the seat neighbors in order to rethink and further develop them. Another advantage is the minimum amount of material required. All that is needed here are just six pens and six prepared sheets of paper, each divided into three columns and six rows. After each participant has received one of the sheets, you introduce the task to be worked on, explain the rules and are responsible for keeping to the specified time. Each of the six rounds is scheduled to take between three and five minutes. The first of six rounds can now begin. Each participant has the task of spontaneously filling the top three boxes with ideas on the topic. In the next rounds, all the lines are filled in one by one, with the ideas of the previous participants visible and deliberately used as inspiration for further ideas. With the sixth round, all participants receive their own starting sheet back. In practice, such a sheet could look as follows: The question arises as to how the stagnating sales of a product could be increased. After round 1, the top line could look like this: new packaging - introduction of loyalty points - gluten-free variant. In round 2, these three ideas will be further developed in a targeted manner: The packaging could be given a shape that matches the content, the loyalty points could be stuck in a loyalty album, and the health-promoting aspects could be advertised on the outer packaging. In the next rounds, these ideas will then probably be further concretized, expanded and refined. In this way, the 6-3-5 method turns out to be an extremely effective creative technique that is able to generate concrete and unusual ideas with little material and time expenditure. In the further course of the workshop, these ideas can then be discussed, analyzed, evaluated and checked for their feasibility.

ABC list

Using the letters of the alphabet, this creative technique intuitively generates new ideas through free association. Listed vertically on a sheet of paper, the letters from A to Z provide a predefined structure to guide the brainstorming process. Letters such as I and J, O and P or X, Y and Z can also be combined into one line if desired. According to the question, generic terms found by shouting are now noted behind the respective letter. Since several generic terms can be assigned to one letter, the creative process is not restricted at any time. Blank spaces are expressly permitted with this method, also the idea identification does not have to take place at all in the order of the alphabet. The ABC method provides for a time frame of approximately ten minutes and can be accomplished both individually and in the group. After the time has elapsed, the ideas are discussed and, based on the question, a decision is made as to which generic term best fits the given letter in each case. In this way, you generate a pool of creative ideas that you can further prioritize and work on in a goal-oriented manner in the further course.

Mindmapping for networking ideas

Mindmapping is a cognitive technique that allows you to visually open up a complex subject area and present it clearly. With a mind map, you as the moderator create a quasi transcript of a creative exchange of ideas, which will serve as a basis for planning in the further course of the process. The creation of a mind map is determined by many rules and is therefore extremely complex. For this reason, you should only consider mind mapping for your workshop if you are absolutely confident in using this method. A mind map is created on unlined paper on a pin board. In the center is the central theme. Based on this theme, further subthemes are generated in the course of collecting ideas and are connected and graphically represented with the help of key terms, upper and lower case letters, colors, symbols, lines and branches. In this way, a clearly defined structure is created right from the start. Thoughts are sorted immediately, in contrast to purely on-call questioning, where thoughts are first collected and then sorted together. The advantages of this method are therefore clear: ideas are concentrated on the essentials, are arranged hierarchically, grouped into topic-related groups and can also grow further in the further course through branching. Reason enough, therefore, to invest time and learn this technique.

Walt Disney Method

The Walt Disney method is a creative technique based on role-playing and looks at the problem to be worked on from three different angles. It is used in particular when ideas are to be concretized and tested for their practical feasibility. The unusual name goes back to a gentleman named Dilts, who once wrote about the famous film producer Walt Disney: "In fact, there were three Walts: the dreamer, the realist and the sourpuss." The problem is now viewed accordingly from precisely these three perspectives. While the dreamer approaches the problem subjectively and enthusiastically, the realist views the situation much more pragmatically. For him, the practical aspect is in the foreground; his approach to solving the problem lies in clarifying the necessary prerequisites and corresponding work steps. The critic, on the other hand, puts the ideas of the dreamer and the realist to the test. His constructive criticism is intended to specifically draw attention to sources of error, he looks for stumbling blocks, risks, weaknesses and contradictions and in this way contributes to optimizing the course of the process. In the first step, you as the moderator specify the task as concretely as possible. Then the entire team slips into each role one after the other with the aim of being able to assess the situation more comprehensively from three different perspectives. As always, you take on the role of a neutral moderator who attentively follows the thought processes of his participants and visualizes them for all to see. It is important to know that the Walt Disney method is not specifically about finding solutions, but rather aims to loosen entrenched thought structures by taking on different roles.

World Café

The World Café is a method suitable for workshops with twelve or more participants. For you as a facilitator, it is an easy-to-implement method because it requires relatively little effort and professional guidance, yet allows relevant issues to be considered from different points of view. This method proves to be particularly effective with heterogeneous and mixed groups in which all members are affected by the same problem. This is because in the World Café you invite your participants to listen carefully, ask questions, discuss and work together to find a solution to the problem. If you wish, coffee, drinks and snacks will support you in creating an informal working atmosphere that invites a creative exchange of ideas and getting to know each other. With a duration of 45 minutes to three hours, the World Café requires a relatively large amount of time. Four to six people stand or sit at small tables. You have previously covered these with writable paper tablecloths and equipped them with pens. Before you get started, you explain the process and the rules of the World Café to your guests. At each table, a host ensures that new visitors are informed about the content and insights previously developed there. The role of the host should be based on voluntariness. Now, initial questions can be worked on at the tables before a change takes place after 15 to 30 minutes - only the host remains. In this way, the groups constantly remix and a variety of suggestions, ideas and views can emerge, which are recorded directly on the tablecloths with the pens. So, at the end of the creative process, you have tablecloths labeled with many ideas, which you display side by side for all participants to see. The final round of discussion ends at each table with three moderation cards and your request to record on them the top 3 results developed there. You hang these cards on a pin board visible to all participants and have thus already created the basis for the next step: prioritization. If you as a moderator are enthusiastic about the idea of the Word Café, it is recommended that you familiarize yourself thoroughly with it. This is because the method has complex rules, a specific question and a reflection phase that requires a lot of experience from the moderator. For this reason, it would be advisable to first study the World Café theoretically in order to then venture a well-prepared test in practice.

Effective methods for idea evaluation (prioritization).

6-3-5 method, mindmapping, card retrieval, shout-out & co were successful and generated many creative ideas? Your pinboard is filled with labeled moderation cards? Congratulations! But what happens next? As a facilitator, how do you generate the one - most promising - idea? And which method is particularly well suited to your objective? First of all, in the first step, the large number of ideas must be both quickly and strongly reduced through a pre-selection in order to be able to make a fine selection (prioritization) in step two, in the course of which only two to a maximum of 15 ideas will remain. These ideas must now be weighed individually and checked for their usefulness and feasibility. During the entire decision-making process, the only thing that matters is to sort out ideas that are not useful or less useful by weighing up the pros and cons. Ideas that are not suitable are immediately discarded completely without discussion, so that in the end result exactly one idea remains that can then be further developed in the further course of the workshop. As always, as the facilitator, you must be careful not to upset anyone. There will be participants who are very attached to their ideas and are not thrilled when they are sorted out. In such a case, you as the facilitator can always remind them that you are here looking for ideas that will serve the entire group and that, according to democratic principles, should also be supported by the entire group. There is a whole range of methods available for carrying out such an evaluation process, which - depending on the context - you can use simply and effectively for yourself. The scoring method has already been explained in detail in the third chapter and for this reason will not be considered further here.

Simple prioritization methods

There are numerous methods to have collected results evaluated by the whole group. Some of them are quick and easy to implement, others are more complex and require more time. A very quick and effective method is raising a hand. If an idea seems important, the hand is raised; if not, the hand stays down. In this way, an unlimited number of participants can filter out convincing ideas and simultaneously reject less convincing ones within minutes by voting. The same applies to the Thumb Barometer method, where a thumb up stands for full acceptance, a thumb horizontal for neutrality, and a thumb down for rejection. Equally effective is the fist to five fingers method. It offers the great advantage of a wider range of evaluation options and also allows each participant to express not only his or her personal attitude toward an idea, but also his or her individual commitment to realizing that idea. Ingenious! As the moderator, it is your task to explain the meaning of the hand signals in detail beforehand and to ask explicitly before the voting begins whether everyone has really understood the meaning of the individual hand signals. Now everyone raises their hand at the same time, the number of outstretched fingers decides. Anyone who raises all five fingers signals full agreement with simultaneous willingness to actively participate in the implementation of the idea. Raising four fingers does not indicate acceptance alone. Rather, four outstretched fingers signal a desire to continue working on the idea. Three fingers also indicate acceptance, but the willingness to continue working on the idea is correspondingly lower. Two fingers stand for neutrality. Those who raise two fingers like the idea, but at the same time indicate that there may still be a need for discussion. Only one raised finger indicates that no support is to be expected for this proposal because problems would first have to be clarified and changes made. A fist without raised fingers is a clear statement: Veto - proposal rejected!

ABC Analysis (ABC Analysis)

If you face a gigantic flood of ideas, it needs a method, which permits first of all a rough classification. This process is to be facilitated with the ABC analysis by a classification into three classes, which reaches from very important (A) over important (B) up to less important (C). A pin board with already prefabricated ABC classification makes an unproblematic moderation possible here. The participants vote by majority on which idea is to be assigned to the respective categories. There are A ideas, which are regarded as innovative and promising, B ideas, which should be reconsidered, and C ideas, which can contribute little to the total success or miss the goal under circumstances even completely. By assigning letters, participants not only receive a structured overview of the entire topic, but also determine their own focal points that can be worked on in the further course. In this way the total success remains always in the view and can be developed and planned by suitable measures. Thus the ABC analysis turns out as an uncomplicated and flexible evaluation method, which supplies extremely effective results with relatively little expenditure.

Ranking

If the number of generated ideas turns out clearly smaller than with the ABC analysis and if the group does not consist of more than ten participants, also the so-called Ranking can be used. With this method all alternatives are evaluated by each participant first individually and then scored in ascending numerical sequence, the most important point receives the "1", the second most important the "2" etc.. Thus, the sum of all participants results in a weighting of the individual points. However, this method is only useful if the number of alternatives does not exceed seven.

More complex prioritization methods

2, 4, 8 consensus

The 2, 4, 8 consensus method supports groups in agreeing on an idea that will be shared by all participants at the end of the decision-making process. The method takes place in different phases and takes a lot of time. For this reason, it may not be equally suitable for every workshop and for every group. However, the intensive engagement with the issue and the democratic way of decision making are merits that speak strongly for the use of this method. The 2, 4, 8 consensus is designed for eight to 40 participants, and the time required is one to three hours. As the moderator, make sure that you set clear time limits for each phase, and it goes without saying that you are responsible for adhering to them. First, groups of two are formed, to which the ideas previously developed in the plenary session are presented for evaluation. The task of all groups during this phase is to agree on exactly three favorites within the allotted time. In the next step, two groups of two then join together to form a group of four with the goal of reducing the now six common favorites to half through extensive consultation. The next step follows the same principle, except that in this phase two groups of four form a group of eight, which in turn will agree on three favorites. This process continues until the whole group is once again completely united and now, ideally, has to choose the best idea from a selection of only three.

Six Thinking Hats (Six Thinking Hats)

The Six Thinking Hats method is a very complex method that aims at a detailed analysis of ideas. The advantage of this method is that it invites the participants to an interesting change of perspective, which should actively stimulate the exchange of ideas and the abandonment of rigid and entrenched points of view. Here, optimists are allowed to discuss with pessimists, fact lovers with emotional people - and this quite openly and without reservations. This method requires five to 20 participants, and you should allow 30 to 60 minutes. Each of the six thinking hats has its own individual color and tells the wearer in which way and from which perspective he should look at things. Thus the wearer of the white hat takes an analytical position, which is characterized by objectivity and neutrality and is based on data and facts. For the wearer of the red hat, the focus is more on subjective feelings, and his view of things is characterized by personal opinions, interests and prejudices. The characteristics of the wearer of the black hat can perhaps already be guessed here. His view of things is negative; from his pessimistic perspective, he is particularly good at recognizing the disadvantages and errors of an idea, and as a critical doubter, he can point out possible risks and obstacles. The wearer of the yellow hat, on the other hand, illuminates the positive aspects and advantages of the subject, while the tasks of the green hat are to develop completely new, wild and creative ideas, while at the same time searching for possible alternatives. The blue hat is reserved for the neutral facilitator, who also has the task of directing and summarizing all thoughts and ideas. He or she ensures that each option receives sufficient attention without influencing the discussion. In order to record all discussion points on a pinboard or flipchart, it is advisable to have the support of a minute-taker for this method. In practice, you can choose from different variants. For example, the entire group can sit in front of you and discuss the topic, while only individual participants wear hats and participate in the discussion according to their role. On the other hand, the entire group can also first deal with only one hat color and then consider the topic together from all the other "color perspectives" in turn. The latter variant opens up a decisive advantage for you as the moderator: you can plan the order of the hat colors in advance and choose from which angle the topic should be considered first. It makes sense to start a round with the white hat, as it initially deals with the issue in a neutral and objective manner. For the end of a round the blue hat is ideal, since its task is to summarize the results of this round anyway. After so much theory, let's take a closer look at a possible sequence of this inspiring method. The search for ideas is already behind you, now the roles can be assigned. Ideally, you will have brought along six colorful headpieces for this purpose; alternatively, colorful bracelets, buttons or stickers would also be conceivable. These are now handed over to the participants, the meaning of the hat is explained and thus their role is determined. Explain that the hat wearers will now think and discuss in their roles until they take off their hats again. Allow enough time here for everyone to become familiar with their new and unusual roles. Now ideas and issues are considered and evaluated from the appropriate hat perspective, after which the hats move on. The phase ends after all decision options have been worked through or when the allotted time has elapsed. The clear advantage of this method is that by taking on different roles, an openness is created that offers the opportunity to deviate from one's own point of view for once and thus give room to new ideas. Suggestions that would otherwise never have been voiced are heard here. Decisions are weighed up together on the basis of comprehensive argumentation and taken jointly. However, as a moderator, make sure that participants do not identify too much with their new role and that a factual discussion is possibly confused with acting.

Chapter 5: Dealing with challenging persons

Attempt at classification

Participants in a workshop often arrive with clear expectations regarding content and goals. In addition, each individual has his or her own unique (professional) life experience and character traits. Anyone who has ever worked with groups knows all too well that there will always be people with whom cooperation is more difficult than with others. Some participants are too active, nagging and disruptive, while others are too passive, do not participate, refuse to participate and clearly express their unwillingness to participate. Perhaps one or the other person in the room even challenges you deliberately - an extremely unpleasant situation that must be avoided at all costs in order to maintain your authority. Particularly within a workshop, whose task is based on joint work and team spirit, such behavior can lead to undesirable delays or even massive disruptions in the process flow. For this reason, this chapter first attempts to classify difficult participants, before the background and motivation for the corresponding behavior are illuminated in the next step. Only with this knowledge can ways be found to deal with this type of participant in an unagitated and professional manner. Basically, there are five types of difficult participants, which you as a moderator can confront in difficult situations in a targeted and confident manner through good preparation. Do not hesitate to find out in advance who will be attending your workshop. Who could you ask in advance for more information? Conduct short interviews in the course of the workshop that will enable you to classify the people taking part. But how do you tame the know-it-all, the long-talker, the complainer & Co. and what possibilities do you have to use these character traits and to integrate them constructively into the group work? Let's start with the alpha dog.

The leader

The lead wolf is very concerned that everyone in the room knows that he is the undisputed number 1. He may want to interrupt you as the moderator while you are speaking, steer the dialogue in a certain direction, or even usurp it. So what can you do? Should you ignore him? Make it clear to him that you are number 1 here in the room? This probably won't solve your problems because the motivation for his behavior is "power." At worst, he will torpedo your workshop. So you should consider a solution that matches the nature of the lead wolf and gives him the opportunity to live out his alpha behavior. The solution is simple: give him an important task, referring to a later date - "We'll have important decisions to make at various points in this workshop, so we need you." The prospect of a plenary presentation of the results developed in the workshop is also to his liking. If it fits the framework, a mention of the name is also a good idea. This kind of passive recognition leads to sufficient attention; he now no longer has to intervene in the moderation to make himself heard.

The know-it-all

At first glance, the know-it-all seems rather inconspicuous and friendly. But only until he unexpectedly raises his hand and points out that everything here may be going in the wrong direction. In this way, he scatters doubt and uncertainty. But why does he do this? He knows a lot, loves numbers, data and facts, and is simply interested in knowing things better than the others. A good way to deal with the know-it-all is to make him an expert. "That's quite an interesting aspect you raise there. We'll go into that in more detail at a later date, and then we'll also need the advice of an expert." To take the wind out of the know-it-all's sails in advance, you can already include very specific points during the planning of your workshop where the know-it-all can demonstrate his knowledge in front of everyone. You can then refer to these points and let him have his say.

The introvert

The introvert is quiet, does not say much and is not very active. As a rule, however, the introvert has precisely the potential that is so urgently needed for the success of the workshop. So how do you tap into this potential? One suggestion would be to simply tolerate his taciturnity and reticence. You may be able to draw him out by regular eye contact and direct questions about competencies and personal experiences. An exchange of opinions in a round or the accomplishment of a task in a two-person constellation also demands active communication from the introvert. The introvert wants to know exactly what needs to be done and therefore needs very clear instructions. The clearer your instructions, the easier it is to involve the person in the process. "Next, take a piece of paper, you have exactly five minutes, and you want the result to look like this." As you plan your workshop, you can start thinking about the wording of your work instructions ahead of time.

The undecided

"I'm not so sure about that." - "Can we really decide that right now?" Statements like these are typical of the undecided. Now, what does a person who is uncertain need? She needs certainty. An appropriate response might be, "We've now reviewed all the data several times and have come to the present conclusion based on that data." You can get the undecided person on your side by making him feel that everything will be fine.

The complainer

For many facilitators, this is the biggest problem and is probably the most exhausting and challenging type among difficult participants due to his many "buts." "The idea is quite good, but ...", "That may be so with other companies, but ..." His latent criticisms and pessimism are a disruptive factor that should not be underestimated, and they are not the only thing that weighs on the atmosphere. His negative attitude makes it difficult to achieve results consistently and quickly, and spreads discontent and demotivation. To get a grip on the problem, you have to make him an expert - just like the know-it-all. Ask him to communicate his nagging in the first person. "What's supposed to make sense about this solution?" then becomes, "I don't think this solution makes sense!" In this way, a whole new content emerges that you can immediately challenge and also have the group discuss. A smart move! A well-prepared moderator may even be able to take advantage of the negative attitude of the complainer, after all, he or she is looking at things from a very unique perspective and has very unique ideas:

On dealing with disruptive behavior

Of overlong contributions and endless monologues As a moderator, you will usually be pleased if the participants actively contribute to your workshop through lively communication. But what do you do when people can't stop talking and make you uncomfortable with overlong statements and endless monologues? This is a problem that you can specifically avoid as early as the planning stage of your workshop by thinking about formulations that on the one hand tactfully slow down the speaker, but on the other hand also emphasize his or her commitment and the multitude of ideas. If the speech gets too long, take advantage of a cue he used and interrupt him specifically: "Thank you, this cue leads us to another item on the agenda." This is a very effective way of tactfully slowing down the long-winded speaker. In addition, you can point out at an appropriate point during the opening phase of your workshop that each participant will only have a maximum amount of time to speak. You specify the amount, but then you must also use a stopwatch to ensure that the speaking time is adhered to. As a rule of thumb, a lot can be said in a concentrated manner during one minute of speaking time. In this way, you avoid losing the participants' interest in the discussion, do not stray from the topic, deal with all the points on the agenda and keep to the allotted time.

Cool sayings and class clowns

Humorous participants will be extremely welcome guests in any workshop. As long as the group and the moderator do not feel disturbed, an amusing quip can certainly lighten the mood and should be acknowledged accordingly. Laughter allowed! However, if participants feel disturbed, it may be advisable to ask the person for his or her opinion on the subject matter just discussed. In this way, you offer him or her the opportunity to return to the factual level. If the disturbances do not stop after this, or if they become more massive, you can tactfully take a stand or even ask the group directly how they would like to deal with such humorous behavior in the further course. Otherwise, the last alternative will probably be a one-on-one conversation in which you politely but firmly ask for the necessary seriousness.

Interruptions and agitation

You interrupt others, finish their sentences, shout in between or tell them what they have to say on the subject without being asked and without beating about the bush - not a good basis for communication. The explanation for such behavior may be impatience or disrespect, but the bottom line is that it cannot be tolerated by the moderator under any circumstances. A simple but effective solution is to interrupt the interrupter himself: "Thank you for your committed objection, but Ms. Maier was not yet finished with her remarks." Another strategy is to remain silent for a moment after an interruption. With any luck, a group member will comment on the behavior. If not, you have skillfully directed the focus to the disturbance and can continue with your program in a completely professional manner. Troublemakers stir up trouble in a variety of ways: They slide around on the chair, flip loudly through the documents, ask for breaks, roll their eyes, yawn demonstratively, write notes or whisper to other participants - just loud enough for everyone to hear, but not so loud that there would be an interruption. As a result, the disruptor achieves two things with his behavior: he moves into the spotlight and, in the worst case, sabotages the meeting objective in the process. To prevent this, you should integrate him into your moderation. If he notes down keywords and ideas on the flipchart, operates the projector or is responsible for handing out the documents, he is where he would like to be - in the spotlight.

From aggressive behavior and personal attacks

As a moderator, the best way to counter aggressive behavior is to remain calm. You can certainly let the person know that you are aware of the tense atmosphere and at the same time ask about the reasons for their anger. Often, such a direct inquiry - packaged in tactful and moderate words - already leads to a reduction in the agitation level of your counterpart. Hostile participants often feel ignored and quickly interpret harmless remarks as an attack. They then go in search of victims whom they want to annoy and expose with their attacks - they are also happy to choose the moderator. In the case of personal attacks and derogatory remarks, there is little room for maneuver. Since such behavior is completely unacceptable, you must take immediate action. Keep calm, take a tactful stand, and as a last alternative you may only have the option of a one-on-one discussion.

Beware of pigeonholing!

When asking about difficult participants, a self-critical moderator should always take into account that conspicuous behavior may well be due to poor preparation or unprofessional moderation. Also an unfortunate time management or a lack of neutrality on your part can give reason for dissatisfaction. Perhaps one or the other personality structure awakens unpleasant memories of your own past, other participants may even hold up a mirror to you and your reactions may therefore be much more emotional than usual. Always question your actions and the reactions you cause in the group by your actions. For example, a participant arrives late and is sure to get attention. You react humorously, make a joke and the other participants laugh. Does the late participant now have a reason to be on time tomorrow? So again, all that remains to be said is: well thought-out preparation, clear rules of the game, knowledge of human nature and a sound knowledge of conversation and conflict management are the most effective preventive measures against any kind of disruption and thus ensure the success of your workshop. Use the participants' behavior as a learning field, observe which behaviors particularly get on your and other participants' nerves and ask why. Then you can react appropriately in recurring situations and give the participant another important piece of information: "Your behavior is not wanted here in my workshop." One final note: Typing can be quite helpful in understanding (your own) behaviors, preparing for them, and being able to respond appropriately. However, you should be careful not to pigeonhole people too narrowly. After all, putting people into pigeonholes often says more about yourself than about the people you are labeling.

What you should avoid when dealing with challenging situations.

Misunderstandings in everyday interactions usually arise because people generally perceive, assume and evaluate things. If you do this in different ways, misunderstandable situations can arise. Assume the following situation: You are in the middle of the moderation and notice that your participants are getting quieter and quieter, folding their arms in front of them, taking a loud breath, yawning, and maybe even whispering to each other from time to time. All verbal and non-verbal signals are set to LONG WAY. At least this is what you suspect and you may judge such participant behavior as pure disinterest or - even worse - as personal criticism of the quality of your moderation. Perhaps this realization makes you nervous, unsettles you, perhaps you yourself are not fully satisfied with the way your workshop has gone so far. What to do in such a situation? "I notice that the ladies and gentlemen are bored ..." - if you now react to the behavior of the participants by making such a statement, you provide an opportunity for further offence and annoyance, which in the worst case can end in open conflict between you and the group. Once the participants start not taking you seriously or making fun of you, the objective of your workshop is clearly at risk. A much better option would therefore be to first perceive the situation described above, suspect boredom or fatigue, but do not relate the situation to yourself, but evaluate it in a completely different way. What could be the reason for the participant's behavior? Is the current topic possibly to blame or the method? When was the last break? Is there an underlying conflict simmering somewhere? To find this out, simply ask. The participants get space to express themselves, you get answers in return, can recognize the problem and counteract accordingly. Your workshop can only be successful if the communication between you and your guests is right. It is always good to have a plan B, it allows alternative methods and can be adapted to the wishes of the participants at any time. In addition, a cleverly chosen wake-up game can considerably improve the mood, dispel fatigue and make it easier to return to concentrated work in the plenary session.

Becoming unsettled by participants

You have planned your workshop professionally, thought more than thoroughly about the use of suitable methods in advance, have already carefully explained your method to those present, explained the task to them, and everything could be going so well - until the moment when the participants don't quite want to see right away what advantages the method you have chosen is actually supposed to bring. It's a method they don't know, one they may not take seriously, one they may even be hostile to, or in the worst case, refuse to accept. One participant might use the situation to push himself to the forefront and further demotivate the other group members through derogatory remarks - "Are we in kindergarten here?" - or unnecessary discussions. Conflict situations of this kind are probably the greatest challenge for you as a moderator, which you can master individually and only with a great deal of sensitivity. In such situations, you must first gently apply the brakes and openly address the conflict. Make it clear which interests and goals you want to achieve with your method and which advantages result from this method for the group. It would be advisable to have already thought about the appropriate wording before the workshop begins so that you can spontaneously recall it from memory if necessary.

Underestimating group dynamic processes

You are in the middle of the moderation, look around and notice that there is a participant sitting there who is looking at you very critically. Maybe his facial expression shows absolute disinterest, maybe he is angry or tries to show you up with critical questions. As you go along, you will probably find yourself repeatedly turning your focus towards this person to check whether he or she is still looking funny, still looks annoyed, or whether further unpleasant questions are to be expected. It's best to get out of the habit of doing this right away. After all, one of your tasks as a moderator is not to make all the participants happy. Rather, your focus should be on the group as a whole. It is they who are in the foreground, who should be encouraged and supported by you on the way to the group goal. Therefore, in case of disruptive behavior of individuals, you can also rely on the support of the group to a certain extent. If the team already knows each other and an individual member is very conspicuous and disruptive, such behavior usually sets in motion the so-called process of marginalization. "Now don't exaggerate ...", "Now calm down ..." or "Now come down ..." would then be expected comments, which you as a moderator should also definitely allow and use for yourself. What would be the consequence if you interrupt the group's rebuke? Then you would inevitably side with the disruptor (which you probably don't want to do), protect him from the group's criticism, and thereby risk everyone else rebelling against you as moderator as well. So, confidently leave the rebuking to the group and take advantage of the fact that the disruptive behavior of the outsider is also often contrary to the interest of the group.

Reacting incorrectly to strange remarks

You're in the midst of brainstorming, excited about lively participation, and then it comes: the idea that's just totally off. Don't let your astonishment at the unconventional remark show, don't laugh, and under no circumstances let yourself be carried away by a pejorative remark. "What kind of stupid idea is that?" - tactically completely unwise. A better alternative would be to thank the person for the suggestion and ask in what way this suggestion can help achieve the goal. A very smart move would also be to ask the other participants for their opinion - "What do you think of this suggestion?" This way, you stay discreetly in the background, gather new arguments, and ideally avoid having to speak up yourself. A third option would be to refer to your individual feelings as a presenter. For example, you can explain that the approach is quite interesting, but you feel that it is not yet fully developed and needs further discussion. Perhaps there is more than meets the eye in an idea that at first glance seemed completely off the mark.

Concrete procedure for disruptive behavior - step by step.

First, a reassuring fact at the outset: disruptions and conflicts are completely normal during a workshop. After all, people with different views and temperaments come together to work on a given issue. As a moderator, you should plan in advance for the fact that unpleasant situations can arise in this context. Deal with possible scenarios and think about suitable countermeasures that will enable you to achieve the desired effect. If this effect occurs, you can continue with your work as a facilitator. However, if the desired effect does not occur, this will present you with real challenges. So what to do? It's time to give you some effective tools for your practice. How to deal with leading wolves and bored participants and how to stop endless speeches has already been mentioned within this chapter. Therefore, the focus at this point should be on the "real" challenges. When participants do not stop interrupting even after repeated requests, behave openly aggressive towards you or others in the group, question you in your role as moderator or generally doubt the sense of the workshop. These are challenges that you must overcome in any case, otherwise you may have to stop the workshop and your objectives will be jeopardized. When dealing with disruptions, it is advisable to follow a step-by-step model that provides you, as the moderator, with numerous options for conflict resolution, while at the same time focusing on avoiding escalation in any form. Whether it's rustling paper, a quick glance at your cell phone, or quiet whispering - stay calm and ignore disturbances of this kind for the time being. Usually, the problem will take care of itself. Only intervene if other participants feel disturbed by certain behaviors. A friendly glance is usually enough to let the troublemaker know that he has been exposed as such. If the disturbance still cannot be stopped, the friendly look becomes somewhat stricter and a suitable gesture encourages the participant to be quiet or to put the cell phone away. A brief raising of the hand is also a very subtle, but nevertheless extremely effective means. Just keep talking while performing the gesture, the troublemaker will know to whom this gesture applies and understand the meaning: "Stop!" The situation becomes somewhat more serious when conversations no longer want to end, short messages are constantly being written or a call is even taken in the plenum. Now you have to react, a direct address is essential. You could ask a short question: "What exactly is the problem?" or you could specifically address the person by name and ask them in clear terms to be quiet or to turn off their cell phone and put it away.

In this context, also point out the rules that you clearly communicated at the beginning of your workshop and that you uncompromisingly insist on adhering to. If a person continues to be provocative, uses a derogatory or insulting tone, you as the moderator have only one option: interrupt the disruptor immediately - "Then let's resolve the problem right away. Immediately call a break of five to ten minutes and confront the person in question in a one-on-one meeting. Under no circumstances should this take place in a plenary session in front of everyone; conversations of this kind always take place in private and outside the door. Take a deep breath - stay calm - smile! Ask about motivations and what could be done so that everyone can take something away from this workshop. If you get a viable answer, then you can return to the plenary and try to implement the suggestion as best you can as you move forward. However, if the answer does not help solve the problem, ask the following question, "May I give you some feedback?" Now that the disruptive participant is sufficiently heard, he or she will most likely answer this question in the affirmative. Then give feedback about what is bothering you right now and what you specifically expect from your counterpart now. Communicate clearly that a solution to the problem must be found right now and that consequences are to be expected if this is not done. At this point, it is no longer sufficient to merely wish for a change in behavior; you must clearly state your position and, in the best case, reach an agreement with which you can continue your workshop. If no agreement can be reached here either, you can ask whether it makes sense to continue attending at all. In other words: Get rid of this person! Openly aggressive, provocative and destructive participants are a danger to the implementation of any workshop and their behavior must not be tolerated under any circumstances for this reason. Therefore, do not hesitate to consider ejection as a final consequence. After all, what would be the consequence if you did not draw a clear line here and put the troublemaker in his place? Presumably, everyone in the plenum would think that you don't have the situation under control and that you don't know how to do your job. Probably everyone would be waiting for the next provocation and your reaction to it. A situation that completely distracts from the actual topic, calls the entire workshop into question and is stressful for everyone involved. You have probably also reached a point at this point where you are struggling internally with impatience, annoyance and anger. If you break the deadlock by kicking everyone out, they will be extraordinarily grateful for your clear regulation.

What to do in case of mutiny?

A participant bluntly tells you in the middle of your moderation that this workshop is of no use to him at all and that the money for this would have been better invested in a sensible fully automatic coffee machine. What do you do if the group decides not to marginalize itself at this point, but to join in this criticism? True to the motto "You can always do worse", the absolute horror scenario then unfolds before your eyes. You will probably feel completely overwhelmed at first and think about canceling the workshop. If you are not mentally prepared for such a scenario, this will probably remain your only alternative. If you are, there is still a chance to save the workshop and deliver results to your client. Even if these will not necessarily meet his expectations, at least you have fulfilled your mission and can charge your fee for the work done. So, what to do in case of mutiny? First, clearly express through your body language that you are deeply affected by recent events. Try not to appear unassailable and cool, also verbally communicate that you are personally hurt as a person with feelings. This will cause participants to stop drilling down for now. Use this break to make an offer to the group. You would now like to ask each participant the same question and write down all the answers. The question is, "What topic do you think belongs in this workshop?" Now, participants may be ranting about management, structures that don't work, difficult working conditions, or coffee machines that are constantly broken. Ask them to reduce their answer to one sentence and visualize all (!) answers in keywords on a flipchart. While you give the participants a short break, filter out the three to four most important core issues. After the break, the work can continue in plenary, you explain your selection and why you decided against individual topics. "The selection of suitable coffee vending machines is not part of my assignment, so I do not want to discuss this point here in plenary." With the help of a suitable prioritization method (Chapter 4), you can now filter out the most important topic and in this way you have saved your workshop and created an atmosphere in which topics relevant to the participants are in the foreground.

Chapter 6: Questioning techniques

He who asks - leads!

Communication is at the heart of successful collaboration between you and your guests. As a facilitator, you welcome, ask questions, explain, guide, summarize, and specifically support your participants on the path to shared decision-making. Your workshop lives from asking questions. Your questions lead to participants feeling addressed, consciously thinking about an answer and also expressing this answer. Properly posed, questions are powerful tools for stimulating conversation, guiding discussion, and mobilizing participants. For this reason, this guide devotes a separate chapter to them.

Open questions

You want to open a discussion in your workshop and are wondering what technique would be appropriate to give participants enough leeway while providing a wide range of response options? Open-ended questions start with a question word and motivate the respondent to give a longer answer, since they do not even allow "yes" or "no" as an answer. For this reason, they prove ideal for starting a discussion, because they open up insights into the views of your discussion participants without pushing them too far in a predetermined direction. Open-ended questions are also a useful tool for gathering ideas. Workshop participants who have a lot to say may need to be slowed down a bit with this questioning technique, while more reserved participants may need to be encouraged to participate actively. How can we solve this problem now? What is your opinion on this point? What goal do you want to achieve with this workshop?

Closed questions

So while open-ended questions encourage comprehensive responses, closed-ended questions usually allow only two answer choices: "Yes" or "No." You will appreciate closed questions during the process whenever you need to have the participants confirm a fact. Do you agree with this proposed solution as it stands? Can I record it in this way? Are you clear about the advantages of this option? In the context of a discussion, closed questions should be used with caution, because you are asking your counterpart to give a monosyllabic answer and the dialog can easily get bogged down in this way.

Reflective questions

Reflective questions are intended to reconfirm the core message of a statement. Within a workshop, this questioning technique offers you the decisive advantage of using a feedback loop to ensure that you have correctly understood the central point of a statement. This prevents misunderstandings and all participants reach the same level of knowledge. In addition, by using reflective questions, you prove to be a more interested and thus good listener. Did I understand you correctly? A proposal for this has already been worked out? In your opinion, does this mean that this point would need to be discussed again in more detail? Option B has more advantages, you say?

Targeted questions

Targeted questions are used to move the solution process forward. By asking specific questions, you can find out whether the realization of a theoretical approach would also be probable and possible in practice - a not insignificant question on the way to achieving your workshop goal. The targeted question knows how to make clever use of the expert knowledge of individual participants and in this way steers the conversation in the direction you want. Which of you already has experience with this problem? What kind of data do you need to consider when making this decision? Is a solution to the problem completely possible with the resources we have available?

Alternative questions

The alternative question shows particularly clearly that the questioner, with the help of the right technique, is able to steer his counterpart in a very specific direction. This is because, as a rule, the question already provides two possible answers by applying the either/or principle. In order to avoid a "neither nor," both alternatives should be positive for the respondent. In the context of a workshop, alternative questions open up different ways of looking at things and different perspectives, from which different approaches to solutions can develop. However, since it is in the nature of the alternative question to strongly limit the answer options of the respondents, it should be used less in the creative part of the workshop. It is more suitable for the final part, when final decisions need to be made and deadlines agreed upon. Do you think it makes sense to review the results after one month or after three months? In this case, do you support Mr. Müller's or Ms. Maier's argumentation? Do you now decide in favor of alternative A or alternative B? The strongly manipulative side of the alternative question is expressed particularly well in cases where the two answer alternatives do not turn out to be positive for the respondent. From a purely theoretical point of view, a "neither" answer would now be possible and sensible. But is it really? Imagine your boss asking, "Would you like to stay a little longer today, or would you prefer tomorrow?" Used tactically, alternative questions set limits and additionally curtail your counterpart's freedom of choice. After all, you don't actually want to work overtime today or tomorrow, but you can't use the alternative "neither" due to hierarchical reasons without having to fear consequences.

What you should look out for when dealing with questions correctly

As a moderator, one of your tasks is to be able to ask questions professionally. Formulating questions sensibly, adapting them to the purpose and asking them at the right time is great art. For this reason, it makes sense to follow important rules for the successful use of questioning techniques: always ask questions in a way that is understandable, precise and as brief as possible. In this context, be aware that long and verbose questions also lead to long and verbose answers. Make sure that your questions are correctly intoned and always make eye contact with the person in front of you. If a group is sitting in front of you, always include the entire group in the question. Only ask specific questions of individual people if it is clear that they can also give the correct answer to your question. Only ask one question at a time and allow your counterpart sufficient time to answer. NEVER ask if you can ask a question, and NEVER apologize for the fact that you are going to ask a question.

How to use systemic questions to guide the creative process.

At some point in the course of your workshop, you may come to the point where the discussion has just been going in circles for some time. The team seems listless, is no longer making any progress and finding a solution is becoming a distant prospect. Now is the right time for new impulses and food for thought. It is good that you as a moderator have sufficient knowledge about the use and effect of systemic questions. Systemic questions can support you in releasing deadlocked thought structures and in returning to your role as a discussion leader. Depending on the desired function, there are six different types of systemic questions to choose from.

Circular questions

The purpose of circular questions is to provide your participants with a new perspective. A changed view of things from which new ideas and approaches can be gained. The method is so effective because all participants take the point of view of a person directly mentioned in the question. In this way, each participant is invited to leave his or her own perspective for once, to think around the corner and to look at the situation from the eyes of another person. How would the situation look from Mr. Metzger's point of view? How would your boss evaluate this circumstance? What do you think your customers think about this offer? But be careful. By directly mentioning a specific person, this person comes into focus and receives direct feedback. If this turns out to be negative, you must intervene immediately. Because the effect of systemic questions is enormous, and so are their side effects under certain circumstances. For this reason, these questions require a lot of preparation and sufficient practice from you. Only when you feel confident in dealing with systemic questions will you know how to deal with them appropriately and be able to react to possible answers accordingly. By the way, your private environment is an excellent training ground.

Hypothetical questions (What if?)

With hypothetical questions you invite your participants to thought experiments. In all likelihood, you will not generate any tangible results by using this type of question, but what you will generate are new and creative approaches to solutions. Because where limiting factors are suddenly eliminated, new energies and ideas can be released. How would you approach the problem if you had unlimited funds at your disposal? Let's assume that a year has passed and you have achieved all your goals. What would you like to think back on? Suppose you had complete freedom of choice. What would you do?

Solution-oriented questions

Solution-oriented questions are always useful when a discussion is deadlocked and a solution cannot be found due to real existing problems and deficits. Your goal as a moderator must therefore be to return the discussion to a more positive atmosphere that is not solely determined by what is missing and what is not working at all. What problems could already be solved? What would be of absolute necessity for a smooth process? What has gone well so far? With the help of solution-oriented questions, you can support the team in focusing their attention on possible solutions and existing resources. In this way, you achieve two things at once: The basic tone becomes more positive again and previously unused resources can be identified more easily. This is especially true when the team recalls its own possibilities, strengths and talents.

Scaling questions

How would you rate the problem at hand on a scale of 1 to 10? Where the number 1 stands for "no problem" and the number 10 for "absolutely unsolvable". The scaling question is used to put an existing problem into perspective. After all, a problem that appears to be unsolvable may appear to be somewhat smaller and more manageable upon closer examination.

Paradoxical questions

How could we drive the project completely against the wall? What would have to happen for your boss to fire you? In what ways could we make the problem worse? Sometimes the most paradoxical questions provide the most creative answers here. Why is that? Well, they confront the group with an existing problem by exacerbating and amplifying it. In this way, space is created for new ideas and approaches to solutions, and for the feeling that the problem at hand could, after all, be much worse. Such idea generation is often accompanied by a large portion of humor, but this does not necessarily mean that serious approaches to solutions cannot be generated.

Wonder questions

Imagine you had three wishes free. What would you wish for? Suppose you were offered your absolute dream job tomorrow. What would change? What if this problem simply disappeared into thin air overnight? Wonder questions can always be used when finding a solution is stagnating and the argumentation is going around in circles. Wonder questions inquire about the desired state and thus draw attention to necessary action steps.

Gender explanation

For reasons of better readability, only the generic masculine form is used in this guide to refer to persons. It should be expressly noted here that the sole use of the masculine form is intended to be understood as absolutely gender-independent. Both female and male readers are equally meant and addressed. In no way does this constitute gender discrimination or a violation of the principle of equality.

Impressum:

Manuel Hausharter wird vertreten duch:
Digital book solution oü
talin